THE PROPHET KING

THE PROPHET KING

A NEW LOOK AT THE HISTORICAL JESUS

RICHARD LAMB

Earth Heart Press
Tallahassee, Florida

6/98   ISBN 0-9657750-0-3

Library of Congress Catalog Card Number: 97-90274

To order additional copies of this book, write to:

Earth Heart Press
P.O. Box 15408
Tallahassee, Florida 32317-5408

V

TABLE OF CONTENTS

Preface

When I was growing up my family went to a Baptist church on Sundays—the First Baptist Church in Tallahassee, Florida. I was a devoted young Christian who took the teaching at this church seriously and sought to apply it in my everyday life. I was baptized, prayed daily, read the Bible, tried to "live a good life" and accepted Christ as my personal savior. In short, I did the things most Christians do.

One Sunday evening, a little girl was standing in front of the congregation, talking about her faith. During the course of her remarks she ended a sentence with, "...I'm going to heaven—I hope!" When she said, "I hope," many in the congregation chuckled. After all, she was just a little girl expressing a natural kind of uncertainty about what the future held for her. After she had finished the preacher stood up and said you should *never*, under any circumstances, doubt or question the *fact* that you are going to heaven. You shouldn't even joke about it. To have these kinds of doubts is to show a lack of faith in God's power and purpose for your life, such doubts are from the Devil, and they should simply not be entertained.

A couple of weeks after this happened another little girl was speaking to the congregation on Sunday night, and I heard her tack onto the end of a sentence, "...because I *know* I'm going to heaven." The preacher smiled approvingly when he heard this, and I'm sure I wasn't the only one who saw a connection between what the preacher had said recently and this little girl's comment.

I never forgot this episode and it made me wonder about the tendency of people to blindly accept what they are told. I felt like it was a form of spiritual and intellectual tyranny to insist that doubts must not be entertained under any circumstances and that the devil was behind such doubts. I could not accept this spiritual paranoia.

As I entered my teens I began to question what I had

been taught about the Bible. I particularly questioned the images of God that portrayed him as angry, jealous and vindictive. I found these images hard to reconcile with the notion that God is our loving, heavenly father. These doubts lead me to reject the traditional view of hell held by the church. I simply could not accept the idea that a loving God would sentence people to eternal suffering because their beliefs or actions didn't meet certain standards.

The responses I got to my questions about hell were totally unsatisfactory. People would say things like, "The consequence of rejecting eternal life is eternal suffering," or, "God doesn't do this to people—people do this to themselves." With these tidy theological formulas they would consign much of the human race to eternal suffering, and would nonchalantly make these assertions as though they were giving a weather report. To me, this was a lot like casually and calmly describing the aftermath of a nuclear holocaust. I thought these people really didn't know what they were talking about.

With all due respect to the good people at the First Baptist Church, I came to feel that the Christianity there was very superficial. I had jumped in head-first and found it too shallow. It was just a lot of people believing what they had been told without questioning it. I know now this characterization is unfair but that is how I saw it. My heart told me to look somewhere else for answers.

When I got to college I majored in religion at Florida State University. I went religion shopping. When I came to Buddhism I found something different and refreshing. The Buddha, who lived in India about 500 years before Jesus, took a couple of commonsense ideas and ran with them. He taught that everything is impermanent and in a constant state of change. Since we humans seek permanent happiness, the result of this constant change is suffering. From this simple observation the Buddha developed a very practical religion.

More than the Buddha's ideas attracted me; his gracious

approach to potential converts was a complete switch from what I had experienced with Christians. The Buddha frequently cautioned people about abandoning their traditions to follow him without carefully considering the implications of their decisions. He told people to try his approach to see if it worked for them. He insisted that experience, not belief, is the overriding consideration in the "holy life."

I was attracted to the Buddha's ideas but I didn't put them into practice until a few years after I'd graduated from college. I started "practicing" Zen, which is a form of Buddhism that emphasizes meditation and, most importantly, enlightenment.

The concept of enlightenment is based on the Buddha's experience in India thousands of years ago. Traditionally, Buddhists have seen the Buddha's enlightenment as an event of cosmic proportions, and to become enlightened is to reach the ultimate state of being.

Zen Buddhists have always quarreled over the relationship of enlightenment to practice, or meditation. To put it in overly simplistic terms, they've argued about whether you "attain" enlightenment or whether you are enlightened from the start. Given my desire for experience, when I started practicing Zen I sided with those who said you "attain" enlightenment. It was the definite objective of my Zen practice. I figured that the experience of enlightenment would resolve any questions I had about my life and its purpose.

I threw myself into Zen with the same enthusiasm I had brought to Christianity. However, my practice led me to the conclusion that the concept of enlightenment was another form of spiritual tyranny; I had put enlightenment on a pedestal and made it into an idol.

When I came to this conclusion I also removed the Buddha from the pedestal I had made for him in my mind. This is because I had always viewed the Buddha's enlightenment just like Buddhists do—the ultimate state of being for humans.

However, as I read the Buddhist scriptures and anything else I could about the subject, and pondered my own Zen experiences, I decided that enlightenment is an inherently mythological concept, as is the notion that a Buddha is the pinnacle of spiritual development.

During this process of struggling with the assumptions I had brought to my Zen practice, I realized I was using the life and teachings of Jesus as a kind of compass to tell me which direction to take; I discovered that, after all my wanderings, this was still my spiritual bedrock. I decided to examine the life and teaching of Jesus anew, with the benefit of the experiences I'd had since my First Baptist days and the vast amount of historical and other information now available. This book is the result of that reexamination.

At first, I felt like I was getting farther and farther away from Jesus. I was getting lost in the details. After a while, though, I started to come back. I felt this powerful figure emerging from the Gospels. Now, I can sense his presence more clearly than I ever could when I blindly followed the path that others took. This has been a very rewarding part of my own spiritual journey, and I'd like to invite you to come along and see for yourself what it is like. This quest for the historical Jesus isn't designed for scholars, but for anyone who has questions to ask and the courage to confront them honestly.

Examining the recorded life of Jesus critically is challenging but it doesn't have to be a destructive process. It can be a process of affirmation, of coming to terms with what is truly in our hearts. What follows is a journal of personal discovery, not a dissertation or historical treatise. It is not for the fainthearted, but neither is it meant to be an attack on anyone's beliefs. I don't expect anyone to agree with what I have to say about Jesus; I just hope I have recorded the sound of his footsteps on at least a couple of the following pages.

FIRST CENTURY PALESTINE

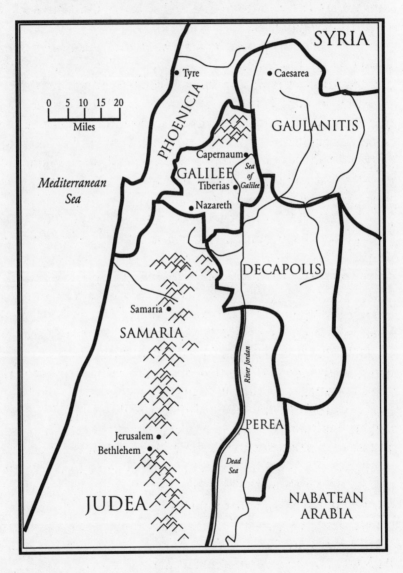

1

THE HISTORICAL CONTEXT

In order to understand Jesus' ministry we must take a look at the historical context within which it occurred. A brief introduction to the history of Israel will be a good place to start because this will provide the background for the Jewish expectation of a Messiah. After discussing this hope for a Messiah I will examine the conditions in Galilee and Jerusalem in the first century, and the features of the religious establishment during Jesus' time. I would also like to discuss the Dead Sea Scrolls and their significance. This historical overview will provide a good basis for the exploration of Jesus' life and ministry that follows.

A Brief History of Israel

Beginnings to Exile:

There is a great deal of uncertainty among scholars regarding the earliest beginnings of Israel. As a measure of this uncertainty, three models have been used to explain the emergence of Israel in Palestine (or "Canaan") and there are serious concerns about each of these models. The first model is the "conquest," which says that Israel entered Palestine from the outside and conquered its inhabitants. This is the oldest model but is currently accepted by few scholars as an adequate explanation for the appearance of Israel. The second model is "peaceful infiltration," which says that Israel was able to enter Palestine peacefully because it settled in largely unpopulated areas. There is considerable archeological support for this alternative, but it doesn't adequately address the likelihood that at least some portion of Israel was indigenous to Palestine. The third, most recent, model asserts that a "peasant revolt" in Canaanite societies led to the formation of a separate ethnic group in the hills of central Palestine, and that Israel was born from these rebellious Canaanites. One problem with this scenario is that we don't have any evidence of a rebellion based on social class during the period in question.[1] Scholars now view these three models as ideal types to be used in synthesis or combination, or they are trying to develop new models for understanding the emergence of Israel in Palestine.

As indicated by the third model above, many scholars now believe a substantial portion of what later became Israel was comprised of displaced Canaanites. These groups left the heavily populated areas of the coastal plains and settled in the sparsely populated central hills of Palestine. They were probably joined by groups migrating into the area from outside, possibly from Egypt and Syria, but we don't know the extent to which these migrations contributed to the composition of Israel.

The settlement by Israel in the central hills occurred at the beginning of the Iron Age, from 1300 to 1200 BCE. (BCE means "Before the Common Era," or "Before Christ") The presence of a group of people called Israel in the region around 1200 BCE is confirmed by the Merneptah Stele. Upon this large granite slab is a hieroglyphic record of the Egyptian Pharaoh Merneptah's military exploits at this time, which specifically mentions a people in Palestine called Israel. Consequently, there was an identifiable group of people known as Israel around 1200 BCE. Although Israel settled in the central hills in large numbers between 1300 and 1200 BCE, we should keep in mind that, generally, the emergence of a separate people in an area is the culmination of a process covering many centuries, and the emergence of Israel as an identifiable group of people is no different.[2]

From the biblical accounts you might get the impression that the Israelites eradicated or subjugated their Canaanite neighbors. In fact, Israel was never more than a minority presence in Palestine, and many areas remained under Canaanite control for centuries after the Israelites settled in the central hills.[3]

The various tribes of Israel kept to themselves for the most part and came together only to fight threats to their security from the outside. Usually, they were rallied by individuals known as "Judges," under whose leadership the united tribes fought.[4]

Whenever the Israelites became involved with Canaanite religions they tended to lose their cohesiveness; they began to blend in with the locals. This made them more vulnerable to attack from outsiders. Conversely, when they rallied around the Judges to fight as the people of Yahweh, the God of Israel, they were much stronger. Consequently, "Canaanites profited by Israelite unity, and this fact, more than any other, enabled the Hebrews to impose on the whole land in large measure a Yahwistic pattern of living. It may be said that the Hebrews conquered Palestine not by destroying their predecessors, but by defending them."[5]

The alliances formed by the Judges were often effective at defending Israel, but were unable to provide the unity necessary to deal with Israel's most formidable opponent—the Philistines. These Aegean peoples were driven from the northeastern Mediterranean during the Trojan wars, and migrated by land and sea towards Egypt.[6] They settled along the southern coastal plain of Palestine about the same time the Israelites were moving into the central hills. During the next two centuries the Philistines conquered much of western Palestine, along the coastal areas and eastward into the hills occupied by Israel. According to the Bible, the Philistines even took the ark of the covenant as booty after the battle of Ebenezer (1 Samuel 4.11). Part of the reason for the Philistines' success was their superior metalworking skills, which allowed them to make iron weapons the Israelites didn't have.[7]

The need for unity in the face of the Philistine threat led to the creation of the Israelite monarchy. The first Israelite king, Saul, a Benjamite, was anointed by the prophet Samuel around 1030 BCE. Soon, he led a general uprising and was able to push the Philistines back to the coastal areas. However, Saul and most of his sons were killed in battle and the Philistines regained control of the territory they had lost. Then, soon after Saul was killed his last son was murdered.[8]

After the death of Saul and his sons, a former warrior in Saul's army named David was crowned king around 1000 BCE. David captured the walled fortress of Jerusalem and made it his new capital city. This was a brilliant move that helped unite the eleven northern tribes and the southern tribe of Judah into one nation.

David, of the tribe of Judah, conquered all of western Palestine and broke the domination of the Philistines in the region. He was a military and political genius who subjugated or formed alliances with his neighbors to the east and north, which provided Israel with a buffer zone for security. The land trade routes between Asia Minor and Africa ran through David's territories and from this trade he was able to extract an enormous amount of wealth. Thus, Israel was secure and prosperous during David's reign.[9]

Upon David's death a palace revolution put his young son Solomon on the throne over the more popular candidate, Adonijah. Despite his reputation for wisdom, Solomon was an extravagant ruler who lacked his father's political skills. He went on a building spree even as he lost control of the trade routes that financed his government's operations, and bankrupted the country's treasury.[10] He put many of his people into forced labor on his building projects and even traded some of his land (twenty cities in what later came to be known as Galilee) to Hiram, the king of Tyre, for the Lebanese cedar used in these projects.

Among Solomon's building projects was the temple in Jerusalem. This temple has often been called a royal chapel since it was part of a complex of royal buildings.[11]

During Solomon's reign he treated the northern tribes more severely than the southern tribe of Judah, and upon his death around 920 BCE the northern tribes broke away and recognized their own king.[12] They established the city of Samaria as their capital.

The kingdom was divided until 721 BCE when Assyria, which had become the dominant power in the region, entered Palestine and conquered the northern tribes. The Assyrians had a policy of relocating conquered peoples. They relocated many of the people of the north and resettled the region with peoples from other conquered lands. As a result, the eleven northern tribes effectively ceased to exist. Jerusalem and Judah were spared by the Assyrians, but only after enormous tribute was extracted from Hezekiah, the Judean king, and much of Judah's territory taken.[13]

The remnant that was left in the north after the relocation intermingled with the people the Assyrians brought in as replacements. Some of their descendants came to be known as "Samaritans." These people maintained their own traditions, which were based on the Hebrew scriptures, and they established their center of worship on Mount Gerizim near the ancient city of Shechem. As readers of the Gospels are aware, the Samaritans were despised by the tribe of Judah, which remained in the south and had Jerusalem as its cultic center.

During the next century Babylon became the dominant power in the region and in 588 BCE Nebuchadrezzar laid siege to Jerusalem. The city held out for eighteen months but was then destroyed, and many of its inhabitants either killed or taken to Babylon as exiles.[14]

From Return from Exile to the Hasmoneans:

The Jews began to return to Palestine and Jerusalem after 538 BCE, when Babylon fell to the Persians. The Persians gave the returning exiles a fair amount of autonomy (as long as tribute was paid) but the recovery was slow and life was hard for the next couple of centuries.

The Jerusalem temple was rebuilt by Zerubbabel, a descendant of one of the last Judean kings, during the period 537-515 BCE. After it was rebuilt, the temple became the center of economic and religious life in Israel. The country's center of power was the aristocracy of priestly families that grew up around the administration of the temple. For much of the period between the rebuilding of the temple and its destruction in 70 CE ("Common Era" or "AD") this aristocracy would be subordinated to foreign rulers politically, but they usually retained a certain amount of autonomy in religious and economic matters.

When Alexander the Great conquered Palestine in 332

BCE there was very little adverse impact on the region. One notable consequence of Alexander's reign was the establishment of the city of Alexandria in Egypt. This city was to become a center of great learning during its history and a large Jewish community settled there. It is estimated that as many as 200,000 Jews lived in the city by the first century.[15] In all probability it was the Jews of Alexandria who translated the Hebrew scriptures into the Greek version known as the Septuagint.[16]

After Alexander's death in 323 BCE things took a turn for the worse. Alexander's immediate successors in the southern part of his empire, the Ptolemies, constructed a ring of Greco-Macedonian cities around Israel (these cities were later known as the Decapolis, or "ten cities").[17] This ever-increasing hellenistic (Greek) presence caused continuing problems for the Jews of Palestine, who came to be deeply divided over matters of hellenistic influence.

Palestine fell into the hands of Antiochus III, the king of Syria, around 200 BCE, after he defeated the Ptolemies at Panion, on Israel's northern border.[18] Antiochus and his successors, the Seleucids, were zealots in the cause of hellenistic culture. Their rough treatment of the Jews in Palestine hastened their dispersion throughout the Near East. During this time a large Jewish community began to form in Antioch, which was to later become an important city in the spread of Christianity.[19]

After a failed attempt to extend his influence into Egypt, Antiochus IV, also known as Epiphanes, decided to punish the Jews of Palestine, who had tried to take advantage of his Egyptian troubles. He sent a force to Jerusalem, razed its walls, seized the temple treasury, and built a fortress to house a permanent garrison.[20] Even worse, he had altars erected to hellenistic gods all over Judea, and in 168 BCE he put a statue of Zeus in the temple.

The Jews could not tolerate these actions and they revolted under a priest named Mattathias and his five sons. This popular revolt was successful in largely removing the Seleucids from the country by 142 BCE.[21] This led to the establishment of the Maccabean, or Hasmonean, dynasty.

During the years of Seleucid control the high priests had been chosen by the foreign rulers. In spite of their initial concern for the purity of the temple's administration, the Hasmonean monarchy took control of the appointment of the high priest and the process of selection became corrupted, with the office often going to the highest bidder.[22] Later, the offices of king and high priest were actually combined in the Hasmonean ruler.

The Hasmoneans had territorial ambitions just like their more powerful neighbors. Under John Hyrcanus I they took control of Samaria, Idumaea (the region south of Judea), and Galilee. In 128 BCE, Hyrcanus destroyed the city of Samaria and its shrine on Mount Gerizim. He often forced conversion to Judaism in the areas he conquered.[23] Under Hyrcanus' successor, Alexander Jannaeus, the boundaries of the kingdom were pushed even further.

Israel in the Roman Empire:

Israel was ruled by the Hasmoneans until the Roman general Pompey and his legions entered Jerusalem in 63 BCE. The Hasmonean ruler at the time, John Hyrcanus II, retained the high priesthood but was essentially demoted from king to prince under the control of the Romans. The Romans gave the Sadducean families a good bit of control over the administration of the temple and economic matters.

In about 40 BCE the Parthians, Rome's rival in the east, briefly gained control of Judea, but the Romans soon drove them from the region. They removed the Parthians' Hasmonean vassal, Antigonus, and replaced him in 37 BCE with Herod, who was to become known as "the Great."[24]

Herod the Great was an Idumean who was never accepted

by the Jewish people. He was a ruthless king and began his reign by executing most of the Sanhedrin, or Council, which had opposed him ten years earlier when he was governor of Galilee.[25] In addition, he didn't hesitate to murder members of his own family or anyone else he perceived as a threat.[26] He promoted hellenistic culture throughout his kingdom and imposed a crushing burden of taxation on the people to support his many building projects.[27] Herod rebuilt Zerubbabel's temple on a grander scale and had a wall erected around it.

Upon Herod's death in 4 BCE there was widespread rioting and rebellion in Palestine. It took the Syrian legate Varus, with four legions, to restore order, but not before thousands were killed and as many as 2,000 crucified.

After Herod's death his kingdom was divided between his three sons by the Roman emperor Augustus. Antipas was given control of Galilee and the Transjordan, Archelaus was given Judea, and Gaulanitis went to Philip. The "Herod" of the Gospels is usually Herod the Great's son, Antipas.

Archelaus was unable to control Judea so, in 6 CE, Augustus incorporated the province into his empire. He sent his legions to oversee a census and exact tribute. He also gave the Sanhedrin and the high priest more authority so that they could work with the Roman governor to maintain order.[28] These governors were generally Roman military veterans selected from the equestrian order, which was lower than the senatorial order of Roman society. These lower level officials were usually given charge of provinces that were particularly difficult to govern.[29]

By the 1st century CE the Jews living throughout the Roman empire were a significant portion of the empire's total population. On average, Jews may have comprised six to nine percent of the population, and in the eastern provinces may have comprised as much as twenty percent. The total number of Jews may have been as high as 8 million, with 2.5 million in Israel itself, 1 million in Egypt, 1.5 million in Syria and Asia Minor, and the remainder spread throughout various parts of the empire or outside of it.[30]

In 66 CE the Jews revolted against the Romans, but the uprising was not one in which the entire nation rose in revolt. As much as anything, the revolt was a civil war among various factions that struggled for control after the early victories of the war. As a result, the Roman general Vespasian and his son, Titus, who had been sent by Nero to put down the rebellion, found it convenient to take their time marching to Jerusalem. After forces loyal to him invaded Italy and he was recognized as emperor, Vespasian went to Rome and left the Jewish campaign in the hands of Titus.[31]

When Titus finally came to Jerusalem with an army of 65,000 in 70 CE, his siege of the city lasted 139 days. The temple was burned and the city destroyed. Thousands of Jews were put to the sword, many starved to death or were sold into slavery, and thousands more were taken to be killed in theaters for the amusement of the Romans.[32]

After the revolt against the Romans in 66-70 CE, there was another unsuccessful revolt in 132 CE in response to the policies of the Roman emperor Hadrian, who was determined to make Judea a hellenized province. He outlawed circumcision and planned to colonize Jerusalem with Romans. The Jews of Palestine rebelled under Simeon bar Kosiba, who was proclaimed Messiah by one of the more prominent Pharisees of the time and renamed Simeon bar Kochba, or "Son of a Star." After the rebellion was crushed, Jews were forbidden to set foot in Jerusalem, which was renamed Aelia Capitolina, and Jewish settlements in the surrounding area disappeared.[33] The Jewish presence in Palestine was significantly reduced at this time.

Historical Summary:

The story of Israel is a remarkable one. During the time from the Exodus to the Dispersion many nations rose and fell.

During Israel's history, when a nation was defeated in battle its god was defeated also and thus discredited. The religion of Israel was different. When Israel was defeated it was because the people had let down their God, who was punishing them for not living up to their covenant responsibilities. The unique religious expression of Israel proved to be a unifying force that allowed the tribe of Judah to survive as a nation and a people.

The history of Israel is one of struggle. The nation was caught between powerful nations such as Egypt, Assyria, Babylon, Persia, and Rome. The constant oppression Israel endured eventually gave rise to hopes that, one day, God would vanquish the oppressors and restore Israel to greatness. This hope came to be expressed, in the time of Jesus, as the hope for a Messiah.

The Hope for a Messiah

The Hebrew word mashiah, which is translated "Messiah" in English and "Christos" in Greek, means "the anointed." It is a kingly title, based on the ancient practice of anointing kings.

Most Christians believe the hope for a Messiah is an ancient one found throughout the Hebrew Bible (the "Old Testament"), which they see primarily as the foundation upon which the messianic hope was built. However, although the idea of a future king is found as early as the Psalms and Jeremiah, the word "mashiah" is found in the Hebrew Bible only thirty-eight times, and it never refers to a future king. It is used twice to describe the patriarchs, six times to describe the high priest, once for Cyrus (the Persian king who conquered Babylon and released Israel from captivity) and twenty-nine times to describe the Israelite king. Additionally, none of these instances involve the description of an eschatological figure.[34] The closest we get to a future king is Daniel 9.25-26, but the use of the term "mashiah" here is very obscure and is translated "prince" by the New Revised Standard Version. Consequently, in reality, the Hebrew Bible has practically nothing explicit to say about the Messiah.

The messianic hope didn't actually flower until the century or so before Jesus' birth. It may have been as much a reaction to the failures of the corrupt Hasmonean dynasty as to the occupation of Israel by foreign powers.[35] The use of the Davidic dynasty as a model for the Messiah's role may also have arisen during this period, as a challenge to the legitimacy of the Hasmonean rulers.[36]

The scriptural basis of the hope for a Messiah rests not on explicit messianic statements, but those which could be construed as speaking of a Messiah indirectly. Examples are the "enthronement" psalms: Psalms 2, 72 and 110. These are psalms related to the installation of the Israelite king. In Psalms 2 and 110, the emphasis is on God's empowerment of the king, and these psalms talk about his power over the nations in militaristic fashion. For example, in Psalms 2.9-11 we find the following:

"You shall break them [the nations] with a rod of iron,
and dash them in pieces like a potter's vessel."
Now therefore, O kings, be wise;
be warned, O rulers of the earth.
Serve the Lord with fear,
with trembling kiss his feet,
or he will be angry, and you will
perish in the way;
for his wrath is quickly kindled.

Similarly, immediately after the king is called "a priest forever according to the order of Melchizedek," in Psalms 110.5-6 we find the following:

The Lord is at your right hand;
he will shatter kings on the day of his wrath.
He will execute judgment among the nations,

filling them with corpses;
he will shatter heads
over the wide earth.

Clearly, the Messiah derived from passages like these was no suffering servant, but a victorious king who would rule the earth with an iron fist.

Psalms 72 is another enthronement psalm. It emphasizes the king's righteousness and its connection to the land's prosperity. It also states that the king will "live while the sun endures, and as long as the moon, throughout all generations" (Psalms 72.5).

In all these psalms the king is described as one who rules the entire earth and whose reign is everlasting. He is also called God's son. He is a righteous king whose virtue brings prosperity and abundance to his people. The use of such exalted language to describe a king was common practice in the ancient Near East.

Some of the messianic expectations during Jesus' time are illustrated in the apocryphal book called the Psalms of Solomon, which is thought to have been written soon after the conquest of Jerusalem by the Roman general Pompey in 63 BCE. These Psalms refer to the Messiah as "The son of David" and the "Lord Messiah." He is to be a glorified, righteous king who vanquishes the Gentile oppressors and judges the tribes of Israel. He will also be "free from sin" and will reign, not because of his military prowess, but because he relies on God. During the time of this Messiah all the people will be holy and righteous before God.[37]

Messianic expectations in the time of Jesus were not restricted to the hope for a Davidic king who would restore Israel. They included hopes for at least three types of figures: a king, a prophet and a priestly Messiah.

One notable source for the expectation of a prophetic Messiah is Deuteronomy 18.15-19. Here, God tells Moses he, "will raise up for them a prophet like you from among their own people; I will put my words in the mouth of the prophet, who shall speak to them everything that I command" (Deuteronomy 18.18). This originally meant simply that God would speak through prophets so that Israel would know his will, but later formed a basis for the hope of a prophetic Messiah. It also led to the view that the coming of the Messiah (regardless of his identity as a king, prophet or priest) would be preceded by a prophet. This prophet was variously seen as the return of Enoch, Moses, someone like Moses, Elijah, or as a new prophet who had not appeared before.[38]

Another biblical source for the expectation of a prophet at the end of the age is Malachi 4.5-6, which says:

> Lo, I will send you the prophet Elijah before the great and terrible day of the Lord comes. He will turn the hearts of the parents to their children and the hearts of the children to their parents, so that I will not come and strike the land with a curse.

Readers of the Gospels will be familiar with the expectation of Elijah's coming because the early church came to view John the Baptist as Elijah.

The community at Qumran, with its emphasis on ritual purity, hoped for a kingly Messiah *and* a priestly one. The hope of a priestly Messiah doesn't appear to have been that widespread but it was one variation of the idea.

The conception of the Messiah as a future king may have evolved into a kind of superhuman, semi-divine figure who would administer God's kingdom at the end of time—a figure known as the Son of Man. The source for the messianic Son of Man is Daniel 7.13-14:

> As I watched in the night visions,
> I saw one like a human being [son of man]
> coming with the clouds of heaven.

And he came to the Ancient One [God]
and was presented before him.
To him was given dominion
and glory and kingship,
that all peoples, nations, and languages
should serve him.
His dominion is an everlasting dominion
that shall not pass away,
and his kingship is one
that shall never be destroyed.

It seems that scholars have written enough on the seventh chapter of Daniel to fill an entire library. Many interpretations of its visions and background have been offered. This is understandable given the imagery used, the obscure references to historical events, and the apparent importance of this chapter to the Christian Son of Man.

The first thing we should note about Daniel 7.13 is that it doesn't use "the Son of Man" as a title but refers to "one like a son of man." This one like a son of man should be contrasted with the beasts that precede his appearance. Before the one like a son of man appeared, Daniel had a vision of four beasts: the first was like a lion with eagle's wings; the second looked like a bear; the third was like a leopard while the fourth was a strong, terrifying animal with iron teeth and ten horns.

Daniel 7.18 seems to say that the son of man's appearance means, "the holy ones of the Most High shall receive the kingdom and possess the kingdom forever—forever and ever." However, these "holy ones" may be angels or they may be the righteous among Israel.

Even if Daniel's son of man is a corporate figure representing humans or angels, this doesn't mean people weren't able to interpret him as an exalted individual who became identified with the Messiah. This happened in the apocryphal Book of Enoch, which was composed sometime between the second century BCE and first century CE. In this book, the son of man is an exalted figure before whom the righteous are to worship, and through whose name salvation is possible. It is also said that this son of man was "named" before the creation of the world and that he is to be a light for the nations.[39]

Presently, there are doubts that the son of man passages of 1 Enoch were written before the time of Jesus, since they were not found among the fragments of Enoch at Qumran.[40] However, the Son of Man in 1 Enoch, 4 Ezra, and other apocryphal works suggests that this expression, based on Daniel 7, could have been used for a messianic figure during the first century. However, we don't know for certain that it was, or how widespread this usage might have been.[41]

It seems natural that, after suffering under foreign rulers for so long, many Jews would come to feel that only direct intervention by God would bring about the restoration of Israel's sovereignty. It is also possible that, since the Davidic and Hasmonean dynasties did not last, people came to place their hope, not in an earthly king, but in a more exalted, semi-divine figure. As the first century dawned, the view of the Messiah as an earthly king was probably the dominant one, but there were clearly other forms of the messianic hope.

It should be noted that the hope for a Messiah didn't pervade Jewish society in Jesus' time. The Sadducees, for example, had no interest in a Messiah since they were satisfied with their position in society; they just wanted to maintain the status quo. Most likely, the messianic hope was present largely among the dispossessed elements of Jewish society and the anti-hellenistic segments of the population.

During Jesus' time there wasn't just an expectation of a Messiah; there was apparently a succession of messianic contenders. One of these, a man named Theudas, is mentioned in Acts 5.36. Josephus tells us that Theudas was going to lead about 400 followers across the Jordan, after he had parted the waters (like Joshua), but he and his followers were attacked and killed by the Romans. An unnamed Egyptian Jew attempted to lead a band of followers through the wilderness (like Moses) to Jerusalem, where he was to command the walls of the city to collapse.[42] Thus, there wasn't just the hope of a Messiah, there was no shortage of claimants to the title, and many people rallied to the cause of these messianic figures.

Galilee in Jesus' Time

The word "Galilee" means "circle." This name for the province in which Jesus lived is derived from the fact that, as the northernmost part of Palestine, it was encircled by foreign nations (see map on page xi).[43]

At the beginning of the first century, Galilee was a province about fifty miles long and twenty-five miles across. It was bounded on the west by Phoenicia, on the east by the province of Gaulanitis (the Golan Heights), and the Sea of Galilee (a lake eight by thirteen miles in size), from which flowed the Jordan River to the south.[44] To the north was Syria, and Galilee was separated from Judea by Samaria to the south.

Upper Galilee was a hilly region, while the lower part of the province featured flat areas with rich farmland and productive orchards. The Sea of Galilee supported a vibrant fishing and shipbuilding industry. As a result, Galilee was one of the most economically active and heavily populated regions of Palestine.[45]

Nazareth, Jesus' hometown, was a small village in central Galilee about twelve miles southwest of the Sea of Galilee.

Despite Galilee's rich farmland, its people were not prosperous during Jesus' time. Under Herod the Great the populace was forced to support Herod's massive building projects, his payment of tribute to the Romans, and the taxes imposed by the temple establishment in Jerusalem.[46] This high level of taxation continued under Herod Antipas. In addition, the farming methods of the first century were not so efficient that they produced large surpluses of agricultural commodities. What surplus existed was taken by the ruling classes in the form of taxation or bought for export.

Herod Antipas' Galilean building projects included the cities of Sepphoris and Tiberias, built in 6 CE and 18 CE, respectively. Sepphoris had been destroyed by the Romans in 4 BCE, due to its role in the revolt at that time, and was rebuilt as a hellenistic city.[47] Antipas built Tiberias as his capital by the Sea of Galilee. Both these cities were administrative centers for the province and were supported by the surrounding villages.

At the time these cities were constructed, vast regions of the Roman empire were experiencing an economic transition from subsistence farming to cash crops, the increasing use of Roman and other coinage, and the displacement of the peasantry due to the establishment of larger estates.[48] Galilee was also going through this transition as it was integrated into the larger economy of the empire.

The concentration of productive land in the hands of a few wasn't a development that began in Galilee after the entrance of the Romans into Palestine, however. It had begun centuries earlier under the Ptolemies, who treated all their territories as "the king's land." When the Hasmoneans gained control of Palestine many of the larger or most productive estates were brought under the control of the new dynasty. Herod continued the practice of keeping large tracts of the best land for himself and his supporters.[49]

The villages of upper and interior Galilee were probably affected somewhat less by these developments than those in the south. This is because the rugged terrain of upper Galilee, and the Sea of Galilee, tended to isolate the region.[50] Thus, life in these closely-knit communities had been essentially unchanged for centuries at the time of Jesus, although the changes in the region were certainly felt to some extent.[51]

During Jesus' time, Galilee and Galileans were not held in high esteem by Judeans, who viewed the Galileans as backward and uncivilized. This is evident from the Gospels, which contain several statements to this effect.

The City of David

Jerusalem was an ancient city even in Jesus' time. The site on which the city was built had been inhabited since 3500 BCE. About 1800 BCE a large wall had been built around the city, and when David and his forces took it from the Jebusites in 1000 BCE Jerusalem had acquired a reputation for invincibility.

David made Jerusalem his capital and from that time forward it was known as the City of David. In David's time, though, the city was rather small—it had a population of around 2,000 and covered only fifteen acres. It was really little more than a mountain fortress. By the time of Herod the Great, the population had grown to 40,000 people and the city covered 230 acres. [52]

Jerusalem was built on the eastern edge of a ridge that runs parallel to the Jordan River and the Dead Sea. This ridge is actually a large mountain that is sixty miles long (running north to south) and about ten miles wide. Immediately to the east of Jerusalem lies the Kidron valley, and beyond that is the Mount of Olives, which is the extreme eastern edge of the ridge. Farther east, the mountain slopes down about to the Dead Sea, which is almost 1,300 feet below sea level.[53] To the west of the ridge lies the coastal plain, and the Mediterranean is about fifty miles from the city.

During Jesus' time the part of Jerusalem known as the Upper City was home to the city's aristocratic class. Magnificent, multi-storied homes from the first century have been excavated in this area. These excavations tell us that Jerusalem's aristocracy at the time was extremely wealthy.

The poorer inhabitants of Jerusalem lived in what was called the Lower City. This was the city's business district also. The Lower City was located on the southeastern slope of the mountain upon which the Upper City was built.[54]

Jerusalem's situation with regard to its poor was unique in the Roman world. The destitute were generally ignored in cities throughout the empire; charity was not a civic virtue that was widely cultivated. In Jerusalem, however, charity was widely practiced, and among the poor there were many who lived from day to day on nothing but handouts.[55] This kept people from starving but it also created a lot of resentment, and the Tyropoeon valley, which ran through the city, was matched by an economic chasm between the rich and poor.

Since Jerusalem had historically been the political and religious center of the Jewish nation, it had seen a great deal of exposure to hellenistic influence by Jesus' time. Much of the city's upper classes had found Greek culture and ideas powerful attractions, and the city's architecture and social life in the first century reflected this. Additionally, Greek was spoken by a substantial number of the city's residents.[56]

Herod the Great had contributed to the presence of hellenistic influence in Jerusalem. His building projects included an amphitheater for gladiatorial contests that featured wild animals, a hippodrome for chariot races, and a theater for musical and dramatical performances.

The capital was moved from Jerusalem to Caesarea around 6 CE, so Jerusalem had lost some of its political power during Jesus' time. The city was compensated somewhat by the massive rebuilding of the temple, which doubled the size of the temple grounds and took decades to complete.

The temple was the center of Jewish religious life and the frequent pilgrimages to the site provided an important source of revenue for Jerusalem's economy. The temple was also supported by an annual tax imposed on all adult Jewish males throughout the world, and the temple treasury functioned as the nation's central bank. The aristocracy of priestly families that controlled the temple were some of the most powerful families in Jewish society during Jesus' time.

The temple wasn't just the center of Jewish religious life, but was also the engine of Jerusalem's economy. Its tax revenues and tithes supported the army of craftsmen needed to maintain the temple and supply it with the materials used in its ritual activities. The temple's revenues also supported numerous maintenance and construction activities throughout the city. Pilgrims and other visitors supported a thriving souvenir trade and catering industry, and the hides from the sacrificial animals supported local tanners and sandal makers.[57]

Jerusalem was not built along any frequently-used trade routes, but was initially constructed as a mountain fortress. Consequently, what trade there was involved primarily the provision of food for the city, and secondarily the temple's materials and supplies. The materials used in Herod's temple reconstruction were very costly, and included a great deal of imported gold, alabaster, marble and Lebanese cedar.[58]

The primary agricultural produce of Jerusalem was olive oil, and olive trees were planted extensively in the area. Other local crops included grapes, figs and chick-peas.[59] Some wheat was grown in the vicinity also, but not enough to support the city's needs. Consequently, grain was brought in from the surrounding area for use in temple sacrifices, as well as for consumption by the city's residents. A great number of animals were also imported for temple sacrifices and as a food source for the city.

In Jesus' time, Jerusalem was a cosmopolitan city whose economy was based primarily on the temple. As a result of Herod's building program it was a magnificent city, with structures that rivaled those anywhere in the Roman empire. It was also a city that was larger than life, that literally towered over Palestine, and connected the Jewish people to their land and their God.

Sadducees, Pharisees & Scribes

Everyone who has read the Gospels is familiar with the Sadducees and Pharisees, two Judaic groups that opposed Jesus, and each other, during the first century. Modern historical research has raised as many questions about these two groups as it has answered and, given our limited sources of information, we can't be certain when these groups arose, what they believed, what their social status was, or, in the case of the Sadducees, what happened to them. Unfortunately, nothing that the Sadducees may have written about their beliefs or history has survived, so our knowledge of them comes only from individuals or groups who opposed them.

The Sadducees may have arisen as an identifiable group sometime during the Hasmonean period, and they have traditionally been associated with the priestly aristocracy that controlled the temple. However, the Sadducees didn't always control the temple during their existence, and probably had to share power with the Pharisees even when they were the dominant party in the temple administration and the Sanhedrin.

Josephus tells us that the Sadducees were the representatives of the wealthier elements of Jewish society. As such, they tended to be conservative defenders of the status quo. They rejected the doctrine of the resurrection, perhaps because of its implication that there was something wrong with the current state of affairs. The Sadducees rejected the Pharisees' oral tradition and their attempt to integrate ritual purity laws with daily life, since these would also undermine their authority and power as caretakers of the temple.

The Sadducees seem to have disappeared soon after the destruction of the temple in 70 CE. This indicates that they relied on the temple for their power and position. It may also indicate that the Sadducees were discredited by their collaboration with the Romans during their administration of the temple.[60]

While the Sadducees have been seen as the representatives of the wealthy, the Pharisee have often been viewed as the party of "the people." However, this distinction is almost surely too simplistic. The Pharisees were as active in matters of politics and temple administration as the Sadducees (and if they weren't, they certainly wanted to be) and they tended to occupy privileged positions in Jewish society. Although not typically members of the "governing class," the Pharisees were its "retainers," or servants, and filled many positions supporting the upper classes.[61]

The origins of the Pharisees are at least as obscure as those of the Sadducees. Josephus tells us of the Pharisees' political fortunes under the Hasmonean rulers so they were active at this time, but we don't know anything about their activities prior to this.

The Pharisees can be distinguished from the Sadducees in several ways. The Pharisees were more flexible in their interpretation of the law than the Sadducees, and they developed an oral tradition to supplement and interpret the written Mosaic law. Unlike the Sadducees, they accepted the idea of the resurrection. As we can tell from the Gospel accounts the Pharisees, like the Sadducees, had many concerns with purity laws, but the Pharisees invested a lot of effort in their application outside of the temple context. Thus, the Pharisees are often associated with the synagogues, while the Sadducees focused on ritual observance at the temple.

During the decades after the destruction of Jerusalem, the Pharisees began to consolidate their control over the religious life of Israel. Since the Gospels were written during this period, the conflict with the Pharisees they describe is often seen as a conflict with the early church that's been projected back onto Jesus' life. Undoubtedly, there is some truth to this. However, unlike many of the literary creations of the period, which record the experience and views of social elites, the Gospels reflect the experience of marginal social groups. The fact that the Gospels often portray the Pharisees as self-serving lovers of social position may tell us something about how they, and the Sadducees, were seen by many in the lower socioeconomic classes during Jesus' time. The Gospels are also likely to reflect Jesus' view of these groups. Since the priestly classes were capable of hiring thugs to beat individuals who didn't tithe, and hovering over threshing floors to ensure that they weren't short-changed on tithes of grain, it isn't hard to imagine that Jesus had some choice words for the religious establishment of his time.[62]

We should keep in mind that first century Judaism was a diverse, complex phenomenon, and Jews weren't confronted with an either/or choice where the Pharisees and Sadducees were concerned. The vast majority of people probably saw themselves as neither and it is certain that there were other choices available. The community that produced the Dead Sea Scrolls is one example of the alternatives to these groups.

In addition to the Sadducees and Pharisees, the Gospels often mention scribes as opponents of Jesus. Scribes in the ancient world were generally learned individuals who could write (an achievement in those days) and they served in administrative capacities in fields such as government, law, commerce and religion. The Jewish scribes in the Gospels specialized in the interpretation and transmission of the law, and they could have been Sadducees or Pharisees.

The Jewish scribes of Jesus' time came from many different backgrounds. In addition to their scribal activities they often had trades by which they supported themselves. They could come from any social class and be of any racial background. The defining feature of a scribe was not his background, but his knowledge.

Not all Jewish scribes had the same abilities or stature. Some were simply copyists or low-level administrative officials of no distinction. Others were respected teachers who attracted disciples and were venerated by the people because of their knowledge of, and ability to expound upon, the law. At the height of their careers, scribes would tend to be somewhat older than Jesus' thirty or so years, since they often underwent very long periods of training.

The more capable scribes of the Sadducees and Pharisees were some of the heavy hitters of the Jewish religious establishment during Jesus' time. They constituted an intellectual elite that was given the great responsibility of transmitting and interpreting the law. When Jesus challenged members of this group, particularly the more sophisticated scribes from Jerusalem, he was challenging a powerful force in the religious life of his people.

Jesus and the Dead Sea Scrolls

Many scrolls and artifacts were discovered in caves on the northwest shore of the Dead Sea between 1947 and 1956, but "the Dead Sea Scrolls" relevant to a study of Jesus' life are those found in eleven caves around the site known as Qumran.[63]

The Qumran site is a plateau about a kilometer from the Dead Sea. It was the home of a small community of Jews during Jesus' time. There are numerous caves around the plateau that may have been used as dwelling places for at least some members of the community.[64]

The Qumran community may have been founded by priests who broke away from the Jerusalem temple establishment during the Hasmonean period because they believed it had become corrupt.[65] The community was comprised of devout Jews who appear to have deliberately separated themselves from the rest of Jewish society. It was governed by strict rules covering just about every aspect of life, and had many concerns regarding the proper performance of rituals and maintaining "ritual purity."

Many scholars believe that the community at Qumran

should be identified with the "Essenes" mentioned by Josephus, Pliny the Elder, and Philo of Alexandria. However, we don't know for certain that this identification is accurate.[66]

The Qumran settlement appears to have been destroyed by the Romans around 68 CE, and the scrolls in cave 4, of which only fragments remain, were probably dumped in the cave immediately prior to this. However, cave 1 may have been the community's library, since it shows no signs of habitation and the scrolls in this cave were wrapped in linen and stored in jars. Other caves containing scrolls showed signs of habitation and their scrolls were probably being used by the residents when they were abandoned.[67]

The Qumran community looked forward to the appearance of two messianic figures—a kingly one and a priestly one—and it believed these individuals would be preceded by a prophet.[68] These Messiahs were to have fairly traditional roles and weren't to be the basis of mankind's salvation as was the Christian Messiah. Nothing in the scrolls connects Jesus or John the Baptist with any of these figures.

Apparently, the Qumran community believed they were living in the last days before the final, eschatological battle between God and the forces of evil. The most apocalyptic document discovered at Qumran is the War Scroll, which contains detailed descriptions of the military hardware and battle formations to be used in this conflict.[69]

Jesus may visited Qumran but we have no evidence of this; he isn't mentioned in any of the manuscripts recovered from the site. John the Baptist may have been involved with the sect at some point, and his baptism may be related to its practice of ritual washing.[70] The place where John is traditionally thought to have baptized is within walking distance of the settlement.[71] However, there is no direct evidence of John's involvement with Qumran either.

A fair amount of controversy was generated by the restrictions on access to the scrolls imposed by the scholars in charge of them prior to 1991. This led to all kinds of conspiracy theories and wild speculation regarding the content of the scrolls. However, the restrictions on access have been removed and, while all of the manuscripts have not been translated or published, nothing has come to light to substantiate claims that their content is somehow damaging to Christianity or Judaism.[72]

The Dead Sea scrolls provide a wealth of information on Judaism during the period in which Jesus lived. However, it should be noted that there are many unresolved issues related to the Qumran site and its community. These include the identity of the site's original builders and their purpose in constructing its facilities, the period during which the site was first used by the community that left the scrolls there, the identity and motives of the community's founders, and the extent to which the scrolls were actually produced at Qumran. The picture of the community and its history that emerges from the scholarly debate over these issues in the coming years may differ significantly from the "traditional" one sketched above.

2

UNDERSTANDING
THE GOSPELS

In my examination of Jesus' life I'm going to rely almost exclusively on the four canonical Gospels. As attempts by Jesus' followers to understand his life and ministry, these Gospels contain a great deal of interpretive material. Consequently, they must be used cautiously, but they are still our best (in fact, our only) sources of information.

Some insist we must rely, to some degree, on the noncanonical Gospels to arrive at a proper understanding of Jesus' life and ministry. However, the surviving noncanonical Gospels generally were written later than the four New Testament Gospels and they are even farther removed from the historical Jesus. Also, a lot of what has survived is so fragmentary that it isn't particularly helpful. Consequently, I won't use them much.

When reading the Gospels I assume that the teaching they contain is at least remotely connected to what Jesus taught unless I find compelling evidence to the contrary. For example, since Matthew shows more interest in hell than the other Gospels, I could assume that hell is Matthew's concern and not necessarily a concern of Jesus. Similarly, I could assume that Luke's obvious concern for the poor is his invention and not a concern that Jesus shared. However, I take the position that Jesus predicted damnation for the unrepentant, and this was important to Matthew so he emphasizes this feature of Jesus' teaching in his Gospel. Jesus' concern for the poor was important to Luke so he tends to emphasize this aspect of Jesus' teaching. We should just be thankful that Matthew and Luke found Jesus' teaching interesting and reproduced some of it, unlike Mark, who isn't particularly interested in Jesus' teaching, or John, who decided to completely remake Jesus' message to suit his theological interests.

Although I think the concerns of the evangelists who wrote the Gospels are generally related to Jesus' teaching, this doesn't mean I think Jesus said everything attributed to him in the Gospels. Many times, a statement in the Gospels captures something Jesus taught, while altering it or expanding upon it somehow. An example is Jesus' repeated prediction of his death and resurrection. I don't think Jesus made the actual remarks as they have come down to us, particularly as they relate to his resurrection three days after his death. Rather, the statements reflect the church's memory that Jesus expected to die in Jerusalem, that he told his disciples this, and that he predicted his vindication by God at the final resurrection. Similarly, I don't think the detailed instructions to the disciples regarding preparations for the Last Supper go back to Jesus. They simply tell us that, when Jesus went to his final Passover, he went with a planned course of action.

I believe many sayings attributed to Jesus don't actually go back to him in any sense, but are later interpretations of his ministry by the early church. For example, I don't believe Jesus' lengthy monologues in John's Gospel were spoken by him, or that Jesus predicted his "second coming." Also, I don't believe Jesus made the comments in the Gospels about the sacrificial, atoning nature of his death. These are not arbitrary decisions, and the matter of determining the authenticity of a statement of Jesus is something I take very seriously. Consequently, I will explain my reasons for maintaining that a statement isn't original with Jesus whenever I make such an assertion.

Before going further, I would like to discuss the approach to reading the Gospels known as "harmonizing." This approach attempts to reconcile all the Gospel accounts into one consistent narrative. For example, if Matthew says a guard was placed at Jesus' tomb, and the other three Gospels say nothing about this, the harmonizing approach assumes the guard is simply a detail the other three Gospels omitted. No contradiction is seen between the accounts. Similarly, if the synoptic Gospels say that Joseph of Arimathea buried Jesus, while John's Gospel tells us he had help from Nicodemus, it is assumed that Nicodemus really was there. The silence of the synoptic Gospels on this point is not viewed as a contradiction. The details are simply added together to create one picture.

Sometimes, harmonizing isn't simply a matter of adding together details. Occasionally, it becomes a creative method of dealing with contradictions in the Gospels. For example, in Matthew 11.13-14, Jesus is speaking of John the Baptist and says, "For all the prophets and the law prophesied until John came; and if you are willing to accept it, he is Elijah who is to come." In these verses, Jesus states that John the Baptist is Elijah. Yet, when we get to John 1.19-23, John the Baptist is being questioned by some priests and they ask him, "Are you Elijah?" John answers, "I am not." This is a contradiction. If you wanted to harmonize these accounts you could say that maybe John just didn't know he was Elijah when he was being questioned in John 1.19-23. I can't accept this kind of maneuvering. Here we have two different traditions regarding the identity of John the Baptist. That is all. When we acknowledge this we can investigate these traditions and explore the richness of the Gospels, rather than trying to make them into one seamless mega-Gospel.

Harmonizing tends to obscure details that could otherwise provide a lot of information about the traditions recorded in the Gospels. If we can identify these traditions we will learn more about Jesus' ministry and teaching.

The Early Churches

It is often said that the Gospels are creations of the early church. However, it is important to recognize that, during the first century, the "church" was really a number of fairly independent, diverse congregations beset by many questions, disputes and unsettled issues. These issues involved matters of doctrine, church order, rules of conduct, relationships between the various churches, the authority of apostles and other important matters.

Paul's description of the situation in the Corinthian church in 1 Corinthians 11.17-19 gives an example of the conflicts in the congregations of the first century:

> Now in the following instructions I do not commend you, because when you come together it is not for the better but for the worse. For, to begin with, when you come together as a church, I hear that there are divisions among you; and to some extent I believe it. Indeed, there have to be factions among you, for only so will it become clear who among you are genuine.

It sounds like disputes were a typical feature of life in Paul's churches and that things were far from settled. Indeed, the entire first letter to the Corinthians is devoted to resolving one dispute or another at the written request of the church members themselves: abuses at the Lord's Supper, a fixation on speaking in tongues and other "gifts of the spirit," allegiances to different teachers, and other matters (see the reference to their letter at 1 Corinthians 7.1).

Such problems weren't confined to the church at Corinth. In his letter to the Galatians (1.6-9), Paul bitterly denounces the church for straying from his message. He says he is "astonished" that they are "deserting" his Gospel and that anyone who teaches a different version is to "be accursed!" The most critical matter in the Galatian congregation is the matter of circumcision. This matter of whether Gentiles should become Jews before becoming Christians was one of the most divisive issues in the church during the first decades of its existence.

In addition to internal divisions of various kinds, in the first century Christians were persecuted by the Romans and forcefully evicted from Jewish synagogues as heretics. Also, the Jerusalem church founded by Jesus' disciples essentially ceased to exist after the Roman-Jewish War of 66-70 CE. On top of all this, the "second coming" of Jesus (or "parousia") and the dawning of the new age did not occur as expected.

We should consider the effect of the above factors on the composition of the Gospels. First, the Gospels are very defensive and polemical regarding certain things, such as the role of "the Jews" in Jesus' death and Jesus' relations with "the scribes and Pharisees." Also, the Gospels record many different traditions, and layers of traditions. They weren't meant to be theological dissertations that were entirely consistent; they are a record of the religious experience and expression of the first generations of Jesus' followers and the record of his life and sayings as they remembered them. They contain a wide range of theological interpretations of Jesus' ministry. If we don't recognize this we will limit our ability to understand the richness and complexity of these traditions.

Prophecies and Parallels

Christians believe there are many prophecies of Jesus in the Hebrew Bible. Matthew's Gospel alone mentions fourteen of them and many others have supposedly been identified. However, these prophecies can be applied to Jesus only if the original context of the statements is completely ignored. There is nothing specifically Christian about this, because Jews were good at ignoring the context of prophecies in connection with their expectation of the Messiah as well. This doesn't change the fact that the original meaning of the prophecies in question is totally ignored. In my view, when you combine this with the obscure nature of many of the prophecies they lose a lot of their credibility.

We must consider the possibility that the Gospels have "reinvented" the life of Jesus to conform to perceived prophecies. One example of this is Matthew's account of the triumphal entry. First, let's look at the way Mark tells this story (Mark 11.1-3, 7):

> When they were approaching Jerusalem, at Bethphage and Bethany, near the Mount of Olives, he sent two of his disciples and said to them, "Go into the village ahead of you, and immediately as you enter it, you will find tied there a colt that has never been ridden; untie it and bring it..." Then they brought the colt to Jesus and threw their cloaks on it; and he sat on it.

Matthew's version is a little different (Matthew 21.1-2, 4-7):

> When they had come near Jerusalem and had reached Bethphage, at the Mount of Olives, Jesus sent two disciples, saying to them, "Go into the village ahead of you, and im-

mediately you will find a donkey tied, and a colt with her; untie them and bring them to me..." This took place to fulfill what had been spoken through the prophet, saying,

"Tell the daughter of Zion,
Look, your king is coming to you,
humble, and mounted on a donkey,
and on a colt, the foal of
a donkey."

The disciples went and did as Jesus had directed them; they brought the donkey and the colt, and put their cloaks on them, and he sat on them.

Mark's version makes sense, but Matthew gives us this ridiculous image of Jesus straddling two animals as he rides into Jerusalem. Just think about this for a second. Would such a thing even be physically possible? Matthew thought that "the prophet" called for two animals so he provided them; he has remade the life of Jesus to fit his interpretation of scripture. Consequently, a little skepticism seems warranted whenever the fulfillment of prophecies is mentioned.

In addition to prophecies there are many parallels between the lives of Hebrew Bible figures, and the lives of Jesus and John the Baptist. These parallels don't represent the occurrence of predicted events, as do prophecies, but are events that duplicate an occurrence in the Hebrew Bible somehow. Some of the more interesting parallels are as follows:

- John the Baptist wears a leather belt just like Elijah (2 Kings 1.8 and Matthew 3.4).

- In Exodus 1.22, Pharaoh commands that all boys born to the Hebrews are to be thrown into the Nile. Moses escapes because his mother puts him into the Nile in a basket so that he is found and cared for by, of all people, Pharaoh's daughter. In Matthew 2.16-18, the children of Bethlehem are killed by Herod, who has been told that the Messiah is to be born there, but Jesus escapes when his family goes, of all places, to Egypt!

- Elijah goes into the wilderness and, as he is sleeping under a bush, an angel comes and gives him cake and water (1 Kings, 19.1-9). Then, "he went...forty days and forty nights to Horeb the mount of God" (1 Kings 19.8). Jesus also spends forty days in the wilderness: "And the Spirit immediately [after his baptism by John] drove him out into the wilderness. He was in the wilderness forty days, tempted by Satan; and he was with the wild beasts; and the angels waited on him" (Mark 1.12-13).

- Elijah brings a child back to life (1 Kings 17.17-24) and so does Jesus (Mark 5.35-43).

- Elisha fed one hundred men with "twenty loaves of barley and fresh ears of grain" (2 Kings 4.42). After the one hundred men were finished eating, there were leftovers. Similarly, Jesus fed 5,000 people with five loaves of bread and two fish (Mark 6.35-44), and there were twelve baskets of leftovers after everyone had finished eating.

- Elijah was taken up into heaven (2 Kings 2.11), as was Jesus (Acts 1.9-11).

- Joseph's brothers sold him for twenty pieces of silver to the Ishmaelites (Genesis 37.28). Judas betrayed Jesus for thirty pieces of silver (Matthew 26.15).

- In 2 Samuel, David is betrayed by Absalom, who tried to take his place as king. In 2 Samuel 15-18, David crosses the Kidron, a stream or brook, then ascends the Mount of Olives. After forces loyal to Absalom are defeated, Absalom gets caught in a tree and is hanged, before he is killed by some of David's troops. In John 18, Jesus crosses the Kidron valley, beyond which lies the Mount of Olives. He is arrested there and betrayed by Judas. Matthew 27.5 tells us that Judas hanged himself after betraying Jesus.

Both Mark and Matthew have "My God, my God, why have you forsaken me?" as Jesus' last words. This comes verbatim from Psalms 22.1. In addition, the words of the passersby come from the same Psalms:

> All who see me mock at me, they make mouths at me, they shake their heads; "Commit your cause to the Lord; let him deliver—let him rescue the one in whom he delights" (Psalms 22.7-8).

> Those who passed by derided him, shaking their heads. "He trusts in God; let God deliver him now, if he wants to; for he said, 'I am God's Son'" (Matthew 27.39, 43).

It is one thing to say that Jesus' life happened along the lines of Hebrew Bible worthies. It is another to say that the words of the onlookers at the crucifixion essentially duplicated words spoken in the Psalms due to some divine purpose. In such cases it seems that events have been reconstructed using the Hebrew Bible.

These prophecies and parallels were used by Jesus' followers because this was their version of history: Jesus was a prophet, a man of God, the Messiah, and what the scriptures say about him, as such, is obviously the pattern of his life. Accordingly, his life is to be understood using these images and patterns. This reconstruction wasn't done in a deliberate attempt to misrepresent the life of Jesus; it is just how his followers made sense of what had happened. When examining Jesus' life we have to consider the possibility that events in the Gospels are patterned after an expectation based on scripture, not descriptions of historical events.

Early Christian Prophecy and Midrash

We often think of prophecy in connection with the Hebrew Bible, but the early church wasn't just looking there for information about the meaning of Jesus' life and ministry; they were also looking to the prophecies being made by members of the church. This prophetic activity is often ignored but may have played an important part in shaping the church's understanding of its mission and Jesus' ministry.

In the 14th chapter of 1 Corinthians Paul says the gift of prophecy is superior to the gift of speaking in tongues. This is because, when a person speaks in tongues, no one understands what they are saying and no message of value is conveyed to the church. Paul says that when someone speaks in tongues there should be an interpreter so that the church will benefit.

On the other hand, Paul strongly encourages prophecy because it strengthens the church. In fact, in 1 Corinthians 14.1 he seems to indicate that prophecy is the greatest of the spiritual gifts: "Pursue love and strive for the spiritual gifts, and especially that you may prophesy."

In the interests of maintaining order during meetings of the congregation Paul says that only two or three should speak in tongues, that they should speak one at a time, and that there should be an interpreter. If there is no one to interpret, those who would speak in tongues should remain silent. He suggests that the congregation should let only "two or three prophets speak, and let the others weigh what is said" (1 Corinthians 14.29).

With regard to Paul's comments regarding prophecy we should recognize that, in the above verses, he tells us a lot about how he *thinks* prophecy should happen in his churches, not how it *did* happen. Apparently, he felt it necessary to provide some guidelines for prophetic activity in his churches because there were none. Prophecy appears to have been a very unstructured, spontaneous feature of the early church's life.[1]

Some of Jesus' statements in the Gospels may actually have been made by prophets of the early church speaking "in Jesus' name." Doubts have been expressed regarding the extent of these prophetic statements, but some may have found their way into the Gospels. We don't know how much of this has happened because no one has figured out how to distinguish such statements from those made by Jesus.[2]

For purposes of studying the Gospels the Hebrew word "midrash" can be understood as a commentary on, or interpretation of, scripture. It comes in varying types, depending on its function or purpose, but is generally an attempt to relate the message of scripture to the present, or to draw out or expand upon the meaning of scripture in a way that makes its message clearer and more relevant for daily living.

Since the Jewish people believed their scriptures were the sole source of God's revelation to man, great value was attached to interpretations of scripture that elaborated upon its meaning in a creative way, or could derive new meaning from a text. The words of the scriptures were seen as the containers of great mysteries that interpreters could discover and expound upon. As a result, midrash could, many times, go beyond the plain meaning of the text of scripture that served as its basis into a largely unrelated realm of meaning.[3]

Midrash could be a very creative process. It would often incorporate scripture into the body of a commentary in a way that makes it difficult to tell where scripture ends and commentary begins. Consequently, midrash can sometimes appear as an expanded version of scripture.

For purposes of understanding the creation of the Gospels, it is possible to see their authors' utilization of Hebrew

Bible scriptural motifs and themes as a type of midrashic activity. Thus, when we read accounts of events in Jesus' life that contain imagery derived from the Hebrew Bible, we are dealing with what could be called "midrash." Additionally, some of the words attributed to Jesus could be forms of midrash, or expansions upon the original meaning of statements made by Jesus.

We might stop to consider how this midrashic approach differs from what we expect modern biographers or historians to do. For us, it is dishonest to pass off your own words as those of someone else. However, the writers of the Gospels saw their role in the transmission of the traditions they received a little differently. Clearly these writers felt free, at least to some extent, to edit, expand upon, delete, or otherwise manipulate the information they used. In light of this fact, when we read the Gospels we have to consider the possibility that we may be reading the author's commentary, or midrash, on a subject that interests him, and not an objective account of a historical event or saying of Jesus.

A word of caution is necessary with regard to the relationship of midrash to the Gospels. The above description of midrash is very general in nature and doesn't address the complexity of this issue in New Testament studies. We shouldn't get carried away with the idea that the Gospels are essentially midrashic, that they are permeated with midrashic interpretations of various Hebrew Bible traditions, or that they contain a large number of statements by Jesus that are actually someone else's midrash. The definition of midrash, its relationship to other types of Jewish scriptural interpretation, the literary forms and techniques typically used in midrash, and the presence of midrash in the Gospels are all the subject of vigorous scholarly debate-and these are only some of the issues involved in this area. Consequently, we should recognize that midrash is not some magic key that will allow us to unlock the secrets of the Gospels.

Pagan Religions and Christianity

Lately it seems fashionable to stress the Jewish roots of the Gospels. However, the Gospels' portrayal of Jesus' life and ministry, and the ritual life of the early church, seem to have been strongly influenced by the "pagan" religions with which Christianity competed in the first century.

The pagan religions' "mysteries" were very popular when Christianity was undergoing its transformation into a religion separate from Judaism. The mysteries usually involved the ritual identification of the initiate with the death and rebirth of a god. This was often accomplished through the ritual consumption of a sacrificial victim, which was identified with the god. Through such a ritual, it was believed the initiate would gain the benefits the god bestowed, such as ecstatic knowledge, the power to do extraordinary things, or eternal life in some glorified world after death.

One popular cult was that of Dionysus, the Greek god of wine. Dionysus was the only Olympian god born of a human mother; he was the son of Zeus, and his mother was Semele, a Thebian princess. Zeus' wife, Hera, had Dionysus killed but he was brought back to life by Rhea, the wife of Cronus, who was the greatest of the Titans. Dionysus then wandered about spreading his knowledge of the vine and his cult to all he met.

The festival for Dionysus took place in the spring and was associated with rebirth, as were many pagan festivals. This festival was often a drunken orgy in which Dionysus' followers would tear apart animals and eat them raw, drink a great deal of wine, and dance wildly to loud music in an attempt to reach ecstatic states. Thus, through the ritual killing of a sacrificial victim and consumption of wine, the revelers were identified with the god.

Another popular cult was that of Osiris, the Egyptian god of vegetation and civilization. Osiris was also associated with rebirth and the coming of spring. Like Jesus, Osiris was killed (betrayed at his "last supper" by his brother Seth) and then resurrected. Like Jesus, he became judge of the dead after his resurrection. Osiris' followers prayed to him in the hopes of being born into his world after death.

One can find a pagan parallel for just about every important event of Jesus' life—the virgin birth, the miracles, the brutal death and subsequent resurrection and glorification—all were common themes found throughout the religions of the Roman world in the first century.

It is no secret that Christianity expropriated dates, images and rituals from the pagan religions it replaced. For example, December 25th was the birthday of the Roman (or Persian) sun god Mithras, and the word "Easter" comes from the name of an Anglo-Saxon goddess named "Eoster." Moreover, the rituals of the mysteries are similar to the ritual identification of the believer with Jesus in what came to be known as the Mass and Communion of the Catholic Church.

This process of assimilation seems to have begun soon after Jesus' crucifixion, and a great deal of it had already occurred when the Gospels were being written. Consequently, when studying the historical Jesus we should be a little skeptical when we find imagery that seems to replicate the world view of pagan religions. The most obvious examples of this are Jesus' words in the Last Supper narratives, and his assertion in the sixth chapter of John's Gospel that one must eat his flesh and drink his blood to attain salvation.

Christians will react with horror to the suggestion that Christianity is similar in any way to the pagan cults of the first century. This reaction is nothing new—the writers of the Gospels were as anxious to stress the Jewish foundation of their religion as modern Christians. However, religions generally must change and adapt to survive, and neither Judaism nor Christianity were immune to the influence of the religions with which they competed for followers. I would simply like to assert that this is a fact of history, and leave the value judgments and hand-wringing to others.

Some Thoughts on Myth and Legend

Many people don't like to use the M-word (myth) in connection with the Bible or the Gospels. They figure a myth is something that isn't true. In fact, a myth is, by definition, something false. I don't see myth this way. The subject of myth and its relationship to religion is a complex one and it deserves a fuller treatment than I'm going to give it, but I would like to make some brief comments on the subject.

I see myth as the way that our mind pictures the world. It is the shape our understanding of the world takes. Myth is shaped by the perception that everything has a beginning, middle and end. It is the garment with which our mind clothes the body of time.

The mythic view of the world has four components: creation, fall, the hero, and consummation. The creation is how we understand the beginning of things. The fall and the hero talk about what happens after the creation, while the consummation deals with the end. These features of myth are universal; everyone wonders how things started and how they will end, and everyone has something to say about what happens in between.

In the Bible all four of these components of myth are vividly expressed. The first chapter of Genesis describes the creation of the world, in which the formless, primeval chaos is transformed into an orderly universe. This is followed by the fall from grace as Adam and Eve are driven from the garden of Eden. Christ is the hero in the Bible and the book of Revelation contains the consummation. I believe much of the Bible's power to change lives is due to the fact that its mythic structure is so magnificently shaped.

This assessment of the Bible's shape as mythical has no bearing on its historicity, or whether it describes things that "actually happened;" the popular "scientific" world view of this century is just as mythical as the Bible's. According to this modern view of the world the creation is called the "big bang." This creation myth is no inspired "Let there be light" version but just a big, mechanical explosion. The fall of man has become an ascent—a gradual, random evolution into something greater. The hero in science is modern man, who is guided by the light of reason. Unfortunately, this hero is a tragic figure whose rationality has destroyed all his gods (except the ones he can buy) and he lives in a universe that will burn out and turn into black, empty space one day. It should be noted that this modern world view can peacefully coexist in the minds of most people with even the most "primitive" religious beliefs.

The four components of myth can be interpreted as a description of a human life from birth to death. The creation is our birth, when things are formless. As we get older, things begin to take shape. We "name the animals," as Adam did; we learn to use concepts and language. We identify "things." The problems start here, because we become an object among objects. This is the fall from grace because, as we learn to manipulate objects, we become manipulated ourselves. The hero is the process of reaching maturity, and his journey represents the development of a personality that is capable of dealing with things and surviving. The consummation is death, that ultimate mystery that we ponder with so much hope and terror; it is no wonder that the consummation of the Bible, the apocalypse, is described in such terrible, yet hopeful terms.

On the other hand, the four components of the mythic world view may describe, not a process, but a structure. Myth may not describe the life of a person in a linear fashion, but may be a snapshot of our mind at any given time: The creation is the dome of our consciousness, with its unformed potential; the fall represents its particularized objects of awareness; the hero is its conceptual and emotional understanding of our surroundings; and the consummation is that incredible, unfathomable mystery that we know in our heart of hearts is waiting to break through and grab us.

I realize this thumbnail sketch of the wonderful world of myth is incomplete and raises as many questions as it answers. It isn't intended as a definitive statement of myth and its relationship to the Bible, but simply as a suggestion that the topic warrants serious inquiry. I also wanted to bring up the subject because some people believe the story of Jesus is largely a myth. I wouldn't put it quite like that, and I think these people really mean to say that much of what has been written about Jesus is legendary.

This brings us to the subject of legend. A legend is simply a story that is larger than life. Legend often deals with the exploits of the hero in our myths, and the quest or journey is a motif often used to frame legends. Myths may or may not be "true," but legends are necessarily exaggerations. They may be based on actual events, and often are, but they go beyond the facts into the realm of fiction. I believe the life of Jesus as portrayed in the Gospels is chock full of legends: Jesus turning water into wine, walking on water, quieting a storm, raising the dead. These are legends. They may tell us something about Jesus' life, or how Jesus' followers understood his life, but they aren't historical events.

A Summary of the Gospels

To further develop our understanding of the Gospels and the message they were intended to convey, I'd like to summarize the current scholarly thinking on their date, authorship and composition, and add some general notes regarding their content.

Mark

Date, authorship and setting:

The majority of scholars currently believes Mark is the earliest of the four Gospels. However, a vocal minority holds to the older view that Mark was written after Matthew, and possibly Luke, and that the author of Mark made use of one or both of these Gospels.

Most scholars date this Gospel between 66 and 70 CE. Scholars' dating of Mark depends at least in part on how they read the 13th chapter of Mark, known as the "little apocalypse." According to many scholars the wording of Mark 13 implies that the Jerusalem temple had not yet been destroyed. Since Jerusalem and its temple were destroyed by the Romans in 70 CE, it is concluded that Mark was written before this time.

There is a tradition dating back to the church fathers of the second century that this Gospel was written by John Mark, the companion and "interpreter" of Peter. Mark supposedly preserved Peter's memoirs in his Gospel. However, many scholars doubt this tradition is accurate. I find it unlikely that Mark was written by an associate of Peter since, in this Gospel, the disciples are incapable of grasping the most basic features of Jesus' message and the Gospel has an obvious Gentile orientation.

Several places have been proposed for the writing of Mark. The same tradition that identifies the Gospel as the work of John Mark states that it was written in Rome. Other possibilities are Palestine, perhaps Galilee, and Syria.

From Mark 7.3-4 it appears that Mark's Gospel was written for a Gentile audience, because these verses provide an explanation about the traditions of "the Pharisees, and all the Jews." Mark wouldn't need this explanation if his expected readers were Jewish.

Since Mark is considered to be the earliest Gospel, little is known about his sources. Many scholars believe Mark is written in a way that indicates a heavy reliance on the oral tradition of the early church.

It is important to note that some of the oldest manuscripts of Mark end at 16.8, with the women running from the empty tomb in terror. Scholars have concluded that the Gospel originally ended at this point. Apparently, this cliffhanger of an ending was unacceptable and two versions of a more suitable ending were added later. Most Bibles point this out in the text somehow.

Some features of Mark's message:

Mark's Gospel is concerned primarily with Jesus' identity. At its beginning, Jesus is called the Son of God. This seems to be the most important characterization of Jesus in Mark. Although the demons Jesus exorcises know his identity, the only human being to recognize Jesus as the Son of God is the Roman centurion watching his death. In Mark 8.29, Peter states that Jesus is the Messiah, but immediately after this confession Jesus calls Peter "Satan" because he can't understand why Jesus must die. In short, no one in this Gospel, except a Gentile who was involved in his crucifixion, ever figures out who Jesus is!

One of the Mark's themes is that Jesus has been rejected by Israel and embraced by the Gentiles because it is God's purpose. Jesus teaches in parables so that his Jewish listeners won't understand his teaching, and Jesus' disciples are incapable of understanding anything he says. Jesus tries to keep his identity a secret throughout the Gospel (this feature of Mark has come to be known as the "messianic secret"). Jesus constantly tries to keep his healing activity a secret, and when he exorcises unclean spirits he often tells them not to reveal his identity. When Jesus finally does reveal his identity at his trial it brings a death sentence. According to Mark this is the divine plan.

This Markan theme of Jesus' rejection by Israel and acceptance by the Gentiles is told in miniature by a few key verses:

Mark 14.60-63 Before the high priest, the chief priests, the elders and the scribes, Jesus acknowledges that he is the Messiah. In response to Jesus' declaration, the high priest tears his clothes and accuses Jesus of blasphemy.

Mark 15.37-39 As Jesus dies on the cross, he gives a loud cry and breathes his last. Then the curtain of the temple is torn in two, from top to bottom. In response to Jesus' death on the cross, the centurion who is watching declares that Jesus is "God's Son."

What could be more ironic? Before the representatives of Israel, Jesus reveals his identity and is rejected. Dying before a Gentile who has crucified him, he is acknowledged as the Son of God. The high priest's charge of blasphemy, which leads to Jesus' death, is accompanied by the tearing of the high priest's clothes. The death of Jesus on the cross and the recognition of Jesus' identity by the centurion are accompanied by the tearing of the temple veil.

Mark seems fond of allegory. He has Jesus interpret a couple of parables as allegories and tells the parable of the wicked tenants, which is an explicit allegory directed at those who control the temple. It is possible that Mark uses the twelve disciples as an allegorical representation of Israel; they are used to show Israel has abandoned Jesus while he has been correctly understood only by the Gentiles.

Mark's Gospel is not written with a lot of style. It seems to tell a disjointed, awkward, repetitive story. The one-dimensional characters in the Gospel are developed very little. The transitions from one episode to the next aren't very sophisticated. In fact, they are so inadequately developed that episodes are just strung along one after another with the vaguest connections.

This feature of Mark's Gospel is deceptive, however. A careful reading of Mark shows that the placement of events is very deliberate. Mark often wraps episodes around events, such as when he brackets the cleansing of the temple with the cursing of the fig tree and its withering. He also likes to contrast different responses to Jesus, as in his juxtaposition of the stories of the woman who weeps at Jesus' feet, and has her sins forgiven, and Peter's three denials.

Mark gives us very little of Jesus' actual teaching. He is content to say things like "he entered the synagogue and taught" without telling us *what* Jesus taught. Often, when Jesus teaches, his statements are meant to show his identity. Only a few of Jesus' forty or more parables are found in Mark.

Another Markan theme is the controversy that surrounded Jesus' ministry and the opposition he encountered. The controversy starts in the first episode in Chapter 2, when Jesus heals the paralytic who was lowered through the roof of a house and then forgives the man's sins. Some scribes who are present think this is blasphemy. Then, in Mark 2.16, some scribes and Pharisees complain that Jesus eats with sinners. Things get bad in a hurry and when we get to Chapter 3, Jesus heals a man on the sabbath and Mark 3.6 says, "The Pharisees went out and immediately conspired with the Herodians against him, how to destroy him." Obviously, Mark wants to portray Jesus' ministry as a tumultuous affair from the beginning.

Two minor points are worth mentioning: Mark has a few favorite words and images in his Gospel. The reaction of everyone in the Gospel to Jesus' ministry is one of "awe" and "amazement." If Mark had a rubber stamp with the word "amazed" on it he would have saved himself a lot of writing because he uses the word constantly. Also, when reading Mark it is easy to get a little seasick because Jesus always seems to be getting in or out of a boat. In fact, the word "boat" shows up in Mark's Gospel more often than the phrase, "the kingdom of God" (eighteen times to fifteen).

Matthew

Date, authorship and setting:

Among the majority of scholars who feel that Mark is the oldest Gospel, the date of Matthew is thought to be between 80 and 90 CE. There seems to be a reference to the destruction of Jerusalem in Matthew 22.7 and, since Jerusalem was destroyed in 70 CE, many scholars believe a date later than this is indicated.

Matthew reflects a period during which the church is separating itself from Judaism and forming itself as a separate institution, or a time when this separation had already occurred. These factors also indicate a date sometime after 70 CE, when rabbinical Judaism and the church were separating from each other.

Traditionally, the Gospel is thought to have been written by Matthew, the disciple of Jesus who was a tax collector and whose call by Jesus is recorded in Matthew 9.9. However, many scholars question this since the Gospel appears to be a collection of different traditions and not the account of an eyewitness.

Most scholars believe that Matthew and Luke both used Mark as a source, in addition to other material. One reason for this is that agreement between Matthew and Luke begins and ends where Mark's Gospel begins and ends. Additionally, Matthew's Gospel contains about ninety percent of the material in Mark, while Luke contains about fifty percent. Matthew and Luke tend to use Mark's sequence for his material and they use about fifty percent of Mark's actual wording.[4]

Matthew and Luke also share a number of verses not found in Mark, which has led to the view that both relied on a source referred to as "Q" (for the German word, "Quelle," which means "source"). This is a hypothetical source document, a copy of which has never been found. This fact, among others, has led some scholars to question the existence of Q.

This reliance of Matthew and Luke on Mark and Q has come to be known as the "two source hypothesis." There are other theories involving the reliance of one synoptic Gospel on another and they often assert that Matthew is the first Gospel. However, the two source hypothesis prevails among most scholars currently.

Matthew's Greek is better than Mark's and he improves on Mark's wording whenever he uses his material.

A likely location for the composition of Matthew's Gospel is Antioch. Matthew's Gospel records traditions ranging from an early, Palestinian Jewish-Christian church to a later, predominantly Gentile one. The Antioch church was established in the late 30s CE and developed into a Gentile institution over the next several decades.[5] As a result, the church's history would include both Jewish and Gentile traditions, as is the case in Matthew's Gospel.

Some features of Matthew's message:

Matthew contains most of the Gospel of Mark, some material he shares with Luke and his own, unique material, including his birth narratives, which seem to have developed somewhat differently than those found in Luke's Gospel.

The Gospel includes five sermons, one of which is the "Sermon on the Mount." The five sermons correspond, perhaps not accidentally, to the number of books of the Torah, the five books of Moses. Some scholars believe this is because Matthew, who is the most Jewish of the Gospel writers, wants to portray Jesus as a new Moses and Christians as the true Israel. The five sermons are as follows:

Chapters 5-7 (The Sermon on the Mount)
Chapter 10
Chapter 13
Chapter 18
Chapters 24-25

Consistent with Matthew's view of Jesus as a first century Moses, he doesn't see the church as a development separate from Judaism; he sees it as the truest form of Judaism. It is the culmination and fulfillment of the covenant God made with Israel. The Pharisees and caretakers of the temple have rejected God and "the kingdom of God will be taken away" from them and "given to a people that produces the fruits of the kingdom" (Matthew 21.43). To Matthew, this "people" is the church and it includes Gentiles as well as Jews.

We shouldn't go overboard with the assertion that Matthew sees Jesus as the "new Moses," however. Mosaic images are found throughout the Gospels and Matthew would surely prefer "Messiah" or "God's Son" to "the new Moses" as a description of Jesus.

Matthew makes extensive use of the Hebrew scriptures to show that the life of Jesus fulfilled messianic prophecies.

Matthew emphasizes the importance of righteousness throughout his Gospel. In Matthew 7.21-23, Jesus says that righteousness is required to enter the kingdom of heaven, not just prophecies and exorcisms. Also, in the story of the sheep and the goats at Matthew 25.31-46, only "the righteous" enter into eternal life. The emphasis here is not on what people believe, but on their actions.

Consistent with his emphasis on righteousness, Matthew emphasizes God's impending judgment on the wicked and the eternal punishment that awaits them. His Gospel contains several references to fire and punishment.

Matthew seems about as interested as Mark in the "messianic secret." For example, after Peter's confession, in Matthew 16.20, Jesus, "sternly ordered the disciples not to tell anyone that he was the Messiah."

In Matthew 18.6-9, Matthew talks about plucking out body parts that cause you to fall into temptation. Immediately following this he starts talking about church discipline. It appears that the offending bodyparts are members of the congregation who are causing problems, and Matthew's church is going through a period of internal dissension and difficulty with the behavior of its members.

Although Matthew's Gospel may have been written for a mostly Gentile congregation, it records traditions from a period when the church didn't include any Gentiles. An example of such traditions is found at Matthew 18.17, where we find the statement that, "if the offender refuses to listen even to the church, let such a one be to you as a Gentile and a tax collector." This probably wouldn't have been good guidance in a Gentile church.

Luke-Acts

Date, authorship and setting:

The general consensus of scholars is that Luke and Acts were written by the same individual and that both works were written between 70 and 90 CE, with a date toward the later part of this period most likely. Take a look at the first few verses of these books and you will see one reason why they are thought to have the same author.

Tradition tells us that the author of Luke's Gospel was Luke the physician, who was a companion of Paul (see Colossians 4.14, 2 Timothy 4.11, and Philemon 24). As you might expect, doubts have been raised by scholars about this tradition, as is the case with the traditions related to the authorship of the other Gospels. The biggest problem with the traditional view is the difference in theological outlook between

Luke and Paul's letters. Luke doesn't show much interest in Paul's major concerns, including his insistence on justification by faith, and freedom from the requirements of the law. However, we shouldn't assume Luke shared Paul's theological priorities just because he accompanied him, and he could still be the author of the Gospel bearing his name.

No scholarly consensus exists as to where Luke and Acts may have been written. A number of locations have been suggested—Rome, Antioch, Ephesus among them—but most scholars appear to believe the matter of location will simply remain unsettled.

Some features of Luke-Acts' message:

Luke-Acts revolves around two cities: Jerusalem and Rome. At Luke 9.51, Jesus "set his face to go to Jerusalem," and much of the Gospel is what has come to be known as Luke's "travel narrative." Jesus is constantly coming to Jerusalem but it seems that he never quite gets there; the journey takes ten of Luke's twenty-four chapters. Jesus' mission inexorably takes him toward Jerusalem and his ministry reaches its fulfillment in the events that take place there.

Rome is to Acts what Jerusalem is to Luke's Gospel. At the end of Luke the disciples are told by the risen Christ to wait in Jerusalem until the Holy Spirit comes, and then to proclaim the Gospel "to all nations, beginning from Jerusalem" (Luke 24.47). Acts records the movement of the church from Jerusalem to Rome. It focuses primarily on the mission of Paul to the Gentiles and, by the time we get to the end of Acts, Paul is in Rome preaching the Gospel.

During the 1950s, the German scholar Hans Conzelmann contended that Luke's main purpose was to provide an explanation for the delay of the parousia. He believed Luke's solution to this problem was a three-period "salvation history." The three periods were Israel, Jesus, and the Church, and the parousia was consigned to the distant future. Later scholars have largely rejected this view, but Luke seems to have moved the parousia to the distant future when he talks about witnessing "to the ends of the earth" and preaching "to all nations."

We should recognize, however, that Luke's world was a lot smaller than ours. To Luke the Roman empire was practically synonymous with "the world." After all, he tells us in his narrative of Jesus' birth (Luke 2.1) that, "a decree went out from Emperor Augustus that all the world should be registered." Thus, Luke seems to have thought that, when the Gospel had been preached throughout the world (or the Roman world), the end would come. Since Acts ends with Paul preaching in Rome, it is entirely possible that Luke, like most Christians of the first century, believed the end was near.

In the period between the ascension of Jesus into heaven and the parousia, Luke believed God had sent the Holy Spirit to guide the apostles and the church in Jesus' absence. Thus, Luke establishes continuity between the time of Jesus and his time.

Throughout his work, Luke states that the events he describes—the rejection of Jesus by his people, his crucifixion and resurrection, the coming of the Holy Spirit, the mission to the Gentiles—are necessary parts of God's plan and that this plan is coming to completion in accordance with God's will.

Luke tries to show that Christianity is not a threat to the Roman empire. We get a glimpse of the prevailing attitude towards Christianity throughout the empire when, in Acts 28.22, the Jews living in Rome say to Paul, "we would like to hear from you what you think, for with regard to this sect [Christianity] we know that everywhere it is spoken against." By stressing the nonviolent nature of its message and divine calling of its apostles, Luke seeks to show that Christianity is not the subversive threat to Rome it is feared to be.

Of all the Gospels, Luke's shows the most concern for

the poor and has the most disdain for money and material things. Interestingly, in light of his disdain for material things, Luke's favorite image of the kingdom is a great feast. This motif is prominent throughout his Gospel.

Luke's view of the significance of Jesus' death on the cross has been a source of controversy, because he seems not to emphasize its atoning, "salvic" nature. For example, Luke 24.46-47 implies that forgiveness of sins comes through repentance, not because of Christ's atoning death: "...and he said to them, 'Thus it is written, that the Messiah is to suffer and to rise from the dead on the third day, and that repentance and forgiveness of sins is to be proclaimed in his name to all nations.'" Jesus' death may make forgiveness possible but believing that he "died for your sins" is not mentioned in Luke's Gospel as a requirement of salvation.

All of the Gospels have tremendous value, but Luke's has provided a wealth of information about Jesus' life that isn't found in the other three. Only Luke tells us of the shepherds at Jesus' birth and his birth in a manger. Luke contains several parables not found in the other Gospels, including the parables of the good Samaritan and the prodigal son. He gives us the most extended descriptions of Jesus' post-resurrection activity and the only account of his ascension into heaven.

John

Date, authorship and setting:

The most likely date of composition for John is between 90 and 110 CE. However, many scholars believe that the Gospel is a composite of at least three major segments. The first segment, chapters 2 through 12, is often referred to as the "Book of Signs," and may have been composed around 70 CE. This may not have been an actual "book," but could have been simply a collection of traditions relating to the miraculous nature of Jesus' ministry. The second segment, chapters 13-17, is more hellenistic in emphasis than the first. The third segment is the passion narrative of chapters 18-21. In addition, it is likely that the Gospel was edited, or "redacted," at least once after these component parts were initially joined together.[6]

Traditionally, the fourth Gospel has been considered the creation of John, the son of Zebedee, one of the twelve disciples of Jesus. The Gospel speaks of a "beloved disciple," who has been identified with John. However, few scholars today believe John was the author of the fourth Gospel or the beloved disciple. There are a number of reasons for this, among them the following: (1) though John was a Galilean the Gospel shows little interest in or knowledge of Galilee; (2) John was described in the synoptic Gospels as one of the "sons of thunder" who wanted to call down fire from heaven on some unfriendly Samaritans (Luke 9.54), while the beloved disciple is noted for his loving and gentle disposition; (3) the synoptic Gospels tell us that John was present at the transfiguration and Jesus' eschatological discourse prior to his arrest in Jerusalem, and that he helped prepare the Lord's Supper. Yet, none of these important events are found in the fourth Gospel.[7]

This raises the question: Who was the beloved disciple? No definitive answer has been given to this question, but the community that produced the Gospel may have had a founder with some connection to Jesus, and traditions concerning his testimony were incorporated into the Gospel during its development.

Scholars don't know where the Gospel was written. Ephesus has traditionally been seen as the most likely possibility, but Syria and Palestine also have supporters.

For years, scholars focused on the "hellenistic outlook" of John. However, recently more emphasis has been placed on the Jewish background of the Gospel. The discovery of the Dead Sea Scrolls, with their imagery of light and darkness, along with other similarities in terminology and outlook, has hastened this development.

Some features of John's message:

The Book of John is different from the synoptic Gospels in many ways. The most striking difference involves the method and content of Jesus' teaching. In the synoptic Gospels Jesus teaches using parables and brief, pithy remarks, while in John he uses extended monologues and few parables. In the Synoptics, Jesus' message is the Kingdom of God; in John, Jesus himself is the message. Also, John has none of the exorcisms of the synoptic Gospels and exhibits little of their concern for the poor.

In Mark, Jesus doesn't want anyone to know his identity; he instructs those who recognize him as the Messiah to tell no one. Yet, in John's Gospel Jesus cries out, in the middle of a festival crowd in Jerusalem (John 7.37-38), "Let anyone who is thirsty come to me, and let the one who believes in me drink." This shows the radical difference between the Synoptics and John's Gospel with regard to both the content and manner of Jesus' teaching.

The central theme of Jesus' teaching in John's Gospel is his relationship with God. Again and again, Jesus equates himself with God. He uses a series of "I AM" statements that are designed to show he is on the same level with God. One of the most striking of such comments is found at John 8.58, where Jesus says, "Very truly, I tell you, before Abraham was, I am."

It is obvious that, at some point in its development, John's Gospel was edited for the benefit of Gentiles. John takes the time to translate words, like "rabbi" and "Messiah," that any Jewish person would understand. John also constantly refers to "the Jews," and sometimes writes as though Jesus and the disciples were not Jewish.

From the beginning of John's Gospel the "hour" of Jesus' crucifixion and exaltation is anticipated. In John 2.4, Jesus' mother tells him the wedding in Cana is running out of wine. Jesus responds with the following words: "Woman, what concern is that to you and to me? My hour has not yet come." This orientation is present throughout the Gospel. In a number of dangerous situations Jesus escapes harm "because his hour had not yet come."

Jesus' hour finally comes when, through the disciples, "some Greeks" ask to see him. Jesus seems to ignore the request and responds with a discourse that begins with the statement, "The hour has come for the Son of Man to be glorified" (John 12.23). The moment of his recognition by the Gentiles is the moment at which Jesus decides to fulfill his destiny. This is another indication that the Gospel is directed towards Gentiles and seeks to affirm their status as the true followers of Jesus.

The coming of the Holy Spirit is an important event for John. It is clear from John 16.7 that Jesus must ascend to heaven so he can send the Holy Spirit to guide his disciples in his absence.

The teaching of Jesus in John's Gospel is probably the most repetitive of the four Gospels. Much of it can be summed up in one sentence (John 17.21): "As you, Father, are in me and I am in you, may they also be in us, so that the world may believe that you have sent me." The statement, "I am in you and you are in me," or something like it, is almost like a mantra that is constantly repeated throughout the Gospel.

In John's Gospel, Jesus is an otherworldly, almost ghostly, figure. He is clearly a physical person, but he is about as close to the border between physical and spiritual as he can get—he walks through menacing crowds as though they aren't there, has the ability to easily hide himself or move about secretly, is in complete control of everything at all times, and almost never talks about anything but himself. He doesn't seem like a real person.

This picture of Jesus as an almost otherworldly figure may have contributed to the development of Gnosticism which, generally, tended to contrast an exalted spiritual world with the corrupted world of "the flesh." It also emphasized hidden wisdom that was often revealed by a redeemer. It is possible that the community that produced John's Gospel later split into a Gnostic branch and a more "traditional" school. This split may be reflected in the Johannine epistles, which many scholars believe were written by members of the same community that produced the fourth Gospel.

The Jesus of the Gospel of John, and his message, are so radically different from the synoptic Gospels that both versions cannot be correct. Consequently, *I believe the extended monologues of Jesus in John's Gospel are the creation of the evangelist(s) who wrote (and/or edited) the Gospel, not Jesus, and I won't use them in my discussion of who Jesus was and what he taught.* This is an assumption that will have extremely important consequences for my analysis.

A Note Regarding The Composition of the Gospels:

We might ask why it took so long for Jesus' followers to write the Gospels. After all, Paul wrote his letters fifteen to twenty years before the first Gospel appeared, and Matthew and Luke weren't written until almost sixty years after Jesus lived. The reason is simple: The earliest followers of Jesus thought that he would return shortly and establish God's kingdom on earth. Consequently, they were not inclined to write anything down for future generations.

What made them change their minds and write the Gospels? Clearly, there were traditions in the early church that connected the dawning of the new age with Jesus' prediction of Jerusalem's destruction. When Jerusalem was destroyed by the Romans in 70 CE, the "second coming" did not take place as planned. Instead, the Jews rejected Jesus and turned to the Pharisaic rabbis, who soon consolidated their control over the religious life of the Jewish people and declared the Christians heretics. In addition, the Gospel was embraced by the Gentiles and the church was rapidly becoming a Gentile institution. The original disciples of Jesus had passed away and the church was in danger of becoming cut-off from its historical Jewish foundation. The Gospels then appeared to explain the delay in the parousia, to provide a sense of continuity with the life and teachings of Jesus, and to serve as a guide for the institutional memory of the church. A great deal of reflection was taking place at this time concerning the meaning of Jesus' life, and the Gospels served as a repository for decades of theological, religious and prophetic interpretation of Jesus' ministry.

3

WHO WAS JESUS?

A Few Biographical Details

Before I discuss the ways in which the church came to understand Jesus, I would like to mention a few biographical details.

Jesus' name was not actually Jesus. His name was "Yeshua," and is a shortened form of the name, "Jehoshua," which is translated into English as "Joshua." The name Yeshua means "God is salvation."[1]

Luke 2.1-7 says Jesus was born during a year in which there was a census under Quirinius, the "governor of Syria." Although there was no census of "all the world" during the reign of Augustus, there was a census in Judea in 6 CE. However, Matthew 2.1 tells us that Herod the Great was alive when Jesus was born, and Herod died in 4 BCE. Both Gospels can't be right, so we probably should just assume that Jesus was born between 4 BCE and 6 CE.

Pontius Pilate was governor of Judea from 26 to 36 CE. If Jesus was about thirty years old when he began his ministry, as Luke 3.23 tells us, Jesus was probably executed sometime during the middle of Pilate's term.

According to Matthew, after Jesus was baptized by John, John was arrested and Jesus "left Nazareth and made his home in Capernaum" (Matthew 4.13). This happened before Jesus began to call his disciples, according to Matthew. The first chapter of Mark has Jesus returning to Capernaum after he had begun his Galilean ministry. Mark 2.1 says, "When he returned to Capernaum after some days, it was reported that he was at home." The obvious implication of this statement is that Jesus lived in Capernaum at the time. Consequently, we are told that, at the time he began his ministry, Jesus was living in Capernaum, not his hometown of Nazareth.

From the account given in Mark 2.1-4, it appears that Jesus was in his own home in Capernaum when he healed the paralytic that was lowered through the roof. We usually think of Jesus wandering the Galilean countryside proclaiming his message. It is a switch to think of him sitting in his own home talking to people. Jesus surely went from town to town during his ministry so he could reach as many people as possible, but since the roof of his house may have been removed it probably made sense for him to move around in any case.

When Jesus spoke in Nazareth and was rejected at the beginning of his ministry, the crowds that heard him responded by asking (Mark 6.3), "Is not this the carpenter, the son of Mary and brother of James and Joses and Judas and Simon, and are not his sisters here with us?" In the account given at Matthew 13.55, the people refer to Jesus as, "the carpenter's son." These are only places in the Gospels where Jesus' occupation is mentioned. The Greek word translated as carpenter actually has a more general meaning and could also be translated as "artisan." Thus, a trade involving work with metal or stone, rather than wood, could be implied here.

It is likely that, if his father was a carpenter, or artisan of some type, Jesus did this type of work also. However, we don't know this for certain.

From the description of his family at Mark 6.3, we know that Jesus was a member of a large family. For some reason, Joseph, Jesus' father, doesn't appear in the Gospels after the birth narratives. This is speculation, but it is possible that Joseph died before Jesus began his ministry. It is also possible that, since Jesus was seen as God's son, mention of his earthly father was deliberately omitted from the Gospels.

Greek was the lingua franca of the Roman Empire and the New Testament was written in Greek. However, Jesus probably spoke Aramaic, a dialect of Hebrew commonly spoken in Palestine during his time. Jesus almost certainly could speak at least some Greek, though, because the language had been spoken throughout Palestine for 300 years when he was born. It was used extensively in the region during his time, particularly in the areas of trade and administration.[2] Like many Jews, Jesus probably knew Hebrew to some extent also.

This is about all the biographical information we have about Jesus. The lack of such information in the Gospels indicates that these documents were not biographies in the usual sense, but primarily confessions of faith by the individuals and communities that produced them.

How Did The Early Church See Jesus?

The early church left no stone unturned in its efforts to describe Jesus and understand his ministry. The primary descriptions of Jesus found in the New Testament are (1) prophet,

(2) Messiah, (3) Lord, (4) Son of Man, (5) Son of God, and (6) God himself. I'd like to explore the meaning of these descriptions, and comment on the possibility that Jesus saw himself in these terms.

Jesus the prophet:

Throughout the Gospels Jesus is referred to as a prophet, both by himself and by others as well.

When Jesus is rejected in Nazareth he says, "Prophets are not without honor except in their own country and in their own house" (Matthew 13.57). This statement is paralleled by Mark 6.4 and Luke 4.24. See also John 4.44, where John omits the actual statement but refers to it instead.

When Jesus asks the disciples who people say he is, at least some people believe Jesus "is a prophet, like one of the prophets of old" (Mark 6.15).

When Jesus brings the widow's son back to life at Nain, the stunned onlookers respond in the following manner (Luke 7.16): "Fear seized all of them; and they glorified God, saying, 'A great prophet has risen among us!'" See Luke 7.39 also, where a Pharisee questions whether Jesus is really a prophet because he lets a woman who is a sinner touch him.

In John 6.14, the people respond to the feeding of the 5,000 by saying, "This is indeed the prophet who is to come into the world." In John 7.40, when Jesus talks about living water at the Festival of Booths, some of the people say, "This is really the prophet." Other references in John to Jesus being a prophet are found at John 4.19, 7.52, and 9.17.

In Luke 13.33, Jesus is going to Jerusalem because, "it is impossible for a prophet to be killed outside of Jerusalem." In Matthew 21.10-11, when Jesus enters Jerusalem he is hailed as a prophet by the people. A similar reference is found at Matthew 21.45-46.

As the risen Christ is talking with two disciples on the

road to Emmaus, he asks them what things they are talking about and they say (Luke 24.19), "The things about Jesus of Nazareth, who was a prophet mighty in deed and word before God and all the people."

Clearly, it is the consistent testimony of the Gospels that Jesus was considered a prophet by the people and that he thought of himself as one. Also, there is no indication in the Gospels that this designation is incorrect. However, the prophetic nature of Jesus' ministry has traditionally received little attention, primarily because grander claims were made for Jesus by his followers.

Jesus the Messiah:

This is one of the most important descriptions in the New Testament, but the title has different meanings. As mentioned earlier, the most common meaning of this term is the future king who would restore Israel's sovereignty. This meaning is the basis of the disciples' question to the risen Christ at Acts 1.6-7: "...[the disciples] asked him [Jesus], 'Lord, is this the time when you will restore the kingdom to Israel?' He replied, 'It is not for you to know the times and periods that the Father has set by his own authority.'"

Here, immediately after the resurrection, the disciples are portrayed as still hoping for the restoration of Israel's sovereignty. This idea of the Messiah is essentially nationalistic and political in nature. (We should note that, as indicated by the above verses, the church never gave up on the idea of a kingly Messiah, but simply put off his arrival until a future date.)

Later, as the church came to be comprised of Gentiles, the Messiah became a redeemer of all humankind, not just a nationalistic redeemer of Israel. The Christ, or Messiah, of the letters of Paul is the one through whom all can be saved: "For

Christ is the end of the law so that there may be righteousness for everyone who believes" (Romans 10.4).

Contrary to the picture painted by John's Gospel, where Jesus talks about little besides his messianic identity, the synoptic Gospels indicate that Jesus didn't like to talk about the Messiah. Any time the subject comes up Jesus seems to tell people to drop it. Some of the Son of Man statements in the Gospels may give the impression that Jesus had no reluctance to discuss the matter, but if the messianic Son of Man statements are products of the early church the picture changes dramatically.

We find an interesting statement concerning Jesus' messianic claims, or lack thereof, in John 10.22-24, which reads as follows:

> At that time the festival of the Dedication took place in Jerusalem. It was winter, and Jesus was walking in the temple, in the portico of Solomon. So the Jews gathered around him and said to him, "How long will you keep us in suspense? If you are the Messiah, tell us plainly."

It seems a little odd for the Jews in John's Gospel to ask Jesus to tell them plainly whether he is the Messiah. No one who has read the first ten chapters of this Gospel could have any doubts about Jesus' identity. If the question asked of Jesus above has a historical basis, it would indicate that Jesus did not make any overt messianic claims during his ministry.

Jesus may not have claimed to be the Messiah, but it doesn't appear he denied it either. However, a refusal to deny being the Messiah doesn't tell us what ideas Jesus had on the subject.

I believe Jesus saw himself as the Messiah, but his view of the Messiah's mission and identity differed radically from the expectations of the time. Those of his people who hoped for a Messiah were looking primarily for a king who would rule

Israel and the nations, or even a supernatural being who would come on the clouds of heaven. For Jesus, the Messiah was a servant who would call Israel to God's kingdom. His Messiah was fundamentally a prophetic figure.

Jesus may have refused to discuss the messianic question because it was a distraction from his message of the kingdom, and his reluctance to address the issue may have been based on practical considerations as well: Any overt messianic claim could have led to a disturbance or attempted insurrection that would easily have gotten out of control. Given the volatile situation in Palestine during Jesus' time, it would have been counterproductive for Jesus to have asserted any messianic claims in public.

I would like to make one final note about Jesus and the messianic question. We get the impression from reading the Gospels that, everywhere Jesus went, this was a burning issue for the people he encountered and that everyone was on the lookout for a Messiah. This may not have been the case. It certainly was such an issue for the writers of the Gospels and the early church, but it may not have been the predominant question on everyone's mind during the time of Jesus' ministry.

Jesus is Lord:

This was probably one of the earliest confessions of the church. The word "Lord," or "kyrios" in Greek, and "mara" in Aramaic, has a wide range of meanings, but generally means "master." Thus, the earliest Christians confessed Jesus as their master and Lord and committed themselves to follow in his footsteps. One of the earliest Christian declarations was a statement of hope that the second coming would soon take place: "Maranatha," or "Come, O Lord!" Paul used the designation "Lord" with the following meaning: "if you confess with your lips that Jesus is Lord and believe in your heart that God raised him from the dead, you will be saved" (Romans 10.9).

Jesus' teaching in the synoptic Gospels indicates that he saw God as his sovereign and he expected his followers to do the same. He didn't intend to be an intermediary between God and man, and didn't insist that belief in his resurrection was some kind of litmus test for entrance into the kingdom. Jesus' message was one of repentance and following the will of God.

Jesus the Son of Man:

The title "Son of Man" seems to be the self-designation of choice for Jesus in the Gospels, and it had a very specific meaning in some of the earliest traditions of the church. It was used to denote the eschatological figure who would reign as God's surrogate at the day of judgment, and the sayings in which the title is found often speak of the Son of Man's "coming." There are several such statements in the Gospels, some of the most important of which are as follows:

> Those who are ashamed of me and my words in this adulterous and sinful generation, of them the Son of Man will also be ashamed when he comes in the glory of his Father with the holy angels (Mark 8.38).

> For the Son of Man is to come with his angels in the glory of his Father, and then he will repay everyone for what has been done. Truly I tell you, there are some standing here who will not taste death before they see the Son of Man coming in his kingdom (Matthew 16.27-28).

> For as the lightning flashes and lights up the sky from one side to the other, so will the Son of Man be in his day (Luke 17.24).

> Truly I tell you [the disciples], at the renewal of all things, when the Son of Man is seated on the throne of his glory,

you who have followed me will also sit on twelve thrones, judging the twelve tribes of Israel (Matthew 19.28).

In Matthew 25.31-45, the Son of Man judges the nations in the story of the sheep and the goats. The role of the Son of Man in this description of the judgment is consistent with the verses quoted above.

Some scholars assert that Jesus never used the expression, "Son of Man," and its use was a development of the early church. It has also been suggested that, when he spoke of the Son of Man, Jesus was referring to someone other than himself—he saw the Son of Man as an eschatological figure who would appear on the judgment day. After Jesus' death and resurrection, his disciples identified Jesus with this figure.[3] I would like to direct my attention to the latter position, since the reasons for my disagreement with the former will also be explained.

I don't find the latter view persuasive for a number of reasons. First, it would require us to treat as inauthentic a number of statements in which Jesus clearly refers to himself as the Son of Man. Of course, many of these statements appear to be post-Easter formulations of the church, particularly those, such as Mark 10.33, where Jesus predicts his death and resurrection. However, it is possible that the Son of Man designation is so strongly connected with these predictions because Jesus himself made this connection. The gospels clearly indicate that Jesus expected to die when he went to his last Passover in Jerusalem, and he could have described his impending death to his disciples as the humiliation of God's servant, the Son of Man. Also, the attempts to deny the authenticity of a statement like Luke 9.58 ("Foxes have holes, and birds of the air have nests; but the Son of Man has nowhere to lay his head.") seem a little desperate.

Second, if Jesus had told his disciples he wasn't the Messiah, I doubt they would have decided after the crucifixion that he really was. I find it easier to believe that, in addition to predicting his death in Jerusalem, Jesus predicted that he would, subsequently, be vindicated by God in some fashion. Such a prediction of his vindication could easily have led to the creation of the exalted Son of Man statements by the early church after Jesus' death.

Third, the exalted Son of Man statements generally read too much like confessional statements of the church. They were probably developed during periods in which Jesus was absent and his followers were being persecuted (Mark 8.38, above, is a good example of this).

Finally, the imagery and perspective of Jesus' parables generally seem far removed from those found in the predictions of the Son of Man's coming. This doesn't mean Jesus didn't use the title in the exalted sense found in the sayings above, but it seems more likely that the early church invented the eschatological Son of Man statements. They may be declarations of prophets in the church or simply theological assertions made by the writers of the Gospels or others.

Regardless of the identity of the Son of Man, the predictions of his coming appear to be very old. One indication that they reflect very old traditions is their frequent focus on Israel. Whenever we find a statement about the twelve tribes of Israel we are probably dealing with traditions preceding the entrance of large numbers of Gentiles into the church.

Another indication that these statements represent an older tradition is that salvation is often given to the "righteous" and is based on their actions, not on any confession of faith in Jesus as savior. Of course, such statements are found in Matthew and could reflect his theological interests.

In the Son of Man saying at Matthew 10.23, we find what appears to be a rather early view of the church's mission—one that would make sense only when the gospel was being preached exclusively to Jews in Palestine. As Jesus is sending the disciples to proclaim the gospel to "the lost sheep of the house of Israel" he says, "truly I tell you, you will not have gone through all the towns of Israel before the Son of Man comes." This is the earliest view of "salvation history" in Matthew. It is later contradicted by Matthew 24.14, which says the gospel must be preached to all nations before the end comes.

I believe that Jesus used the expression "Son of Man" in the sense found in Ezekiel, where it simply means "man." Jesus used this expression to stress his commitment to his ministry and his role as God's chosen servant. Jesus didn't just give up his family ties, his work, and his home—he even gave up his name.

Just as Jesus seems to have rejected every image of the kingdom of God that involved exaltation, he didn't choose an exalted title for himself. His use of the Son of Man title was equivalent to his use of the mustard tree as a description of the kingdom: he chooses a humble image, not a grandiose one. Israel expected a glorified king or even a semi-divine savior, but Jesus offered it a carpenter's son from Nazareth instead.

Regardless of how, or whether, the Son of Man title was used by Jesus, the church soon replaced it with titles felt to be more appropriate, such as Lord, Christ, and Son of God.

Jesus the Son of God:

This is probably the most enduring and important designation of Jesus developed by the church, and is the most important title for modern Christians. The title is practically synonymous with "Messiah," and is essentially a royal description; many of the kings of the ancient Near East saw themselves as gods, or sons of gods.

Since Jesus appears to have called God his "Father" it is only logical that his followers would come to see him as God's Son. However, I don't think that Jesus, if he did see himself as the Son of God, attached the same meaning to this title that we find in the later Christological speculations of the church. This term eventually came to mean that Jesus is the preexistent, divine Son of God who was present at the creation and through whom all things came to be made. I don't think Jesus breathed this rarefied theological air, or saw himself in these exalted terms.

Jesus is God:

In the years following his death, Jesus became the focus of religious devotion and primary object of worship for his followers. I say "primary" because Jesus and God somehow managed to share the stage in early (as in later) Christian devotional practice. Additionally, the early Christians insisted their religion was monotheistic, even though they often prayed to Jesus and spoke of him as "Lord." It wasn't so much a question of Jesus being God, it was just that God had delegated authority and position to Jesus. In other words, it was proper to exalt Jesus because God himself had done this, and to recognize and affirm this was to glorify God.

This exaltation of Jesus by God, and the appropriate response for Christians, is described eloquently by Paul at Philippians 2.5-11:

> Let the same mind be in you that was in Christ Jesus,
> who, though he was in the form
> of God,
> did not regard equality
> with God
> as something to be exploited,
> but emptied himself,
> taking the form of a slave,
> being born in human likeness.
> And being found in human form,
> he humbled himself
> and became obedient to the
> point of death—
> even death on a cross.
> Therefore God also highly
> exalted him

and gave him the name
that is above every name,
so that at the name of Jesus
every knee should bend,
in heaven and on earth and
under the earth,
and every tongue should confess
that Jesus Christ is Lord,
to the glory of God the Father.

The statement above is an admonition to the Philippians to emulate Christ's humility, but its theological implications have understandably received a lot of attention. One of the key words in these verses is the word translated "form" in verse six. The underlying Greek word refers to the essential substance of something. Paul implies that Jesus is essentially divine in nature. The next key word is translated as "exploited," also in verse six. It means to seize, to take something by force, or to grab at something in an unlawful or selfish fashion. Thus, Paul is saying that Jesus shares God's nature because he emptied himself of all selfish ambitions and consequently has been exalted by God to the highest station.

The statement that, "at the name of Jesus every knee should bend, ...and every tongue should confess that Jesus Christ is Lord," is very similar to the statement of God in Isaiah 45.23 that, "To me every knee shall bow, every tongue shall swear." This certainly points in the direction of identifying Jesus with God.

The statement in the New Testament that comes closest to saying Jesus is God is probably John 1.1, which says that, "In the beginning was the Word, and the Word was with God, and the Word was God." "Word" is a translation of the Greek "Logos," one meaning of which (to the Greeks) was the principle of reason that gives order to the world, but the Word in John is Jesus.

John's Gospel, generally, with its "I AM" statements, Logos theology, and constant references to being "in God," certainly seems to identify Jesus with God. This was the church's conclusion, but it took about 300 years and numerous "heresies" to iron out the details. The belief that Jesus is God reached its final form with the doctrine of the Trinity. This doctrine, which was formulated at the Council of Nicaea in 325 CE, asserts that God is a unity of three "persons"—Father, Son, and Holy Spirit—and that Jesus is most definitely God. However, I don't believe that Jesus actually taught that he was God incarnate, or that he put himself on God's level.

In the Gospels Jesus sometimes forgives sins, and this is taken to mean that he put himself on the same level as God. An example is the healing of the paralytic in Mark 2.1-12, which is paralleled at Matthew 9.2-8 and Luke 5.17-26. Since Mark apparently inserted the forgiveness of sins controversy in verses 5b-10 into this episode, I have separated it from the original story and put the original story in italics:

When he returned to Capernaum after some days, it was reported that he was at home. So many gathered around that there was no longer room for them, not even in front of the door; and he was speaking the word to them. Then some people came, bringing to him a paralyzed man, carried by four of them. And when they could not bring him to Jesus because of the crowd, they removed the roof above him; and after having dug through it, they let down the mat on which the paralytic lay. When Jesus saw their faith, he said to the paralytic,

"Son, your sins are forgiven." Now some of the scribes were sitting there, questioning in their hearts, "Why does this fellow speak in this way? It is blasphemy! Who can forgive sins but God alone!" At once Jesus perceived in his spirit that they were discussing these questions among themselves; and he said to them, "Why do you raise such questions in your hearts? Which is easier, to say to the paralytic, 'Your sins are forgiven,' or to say, 'Stand up and take your mat and walk.'? But so that you may know that the Son of Man has authority on earth to forgive sins"—he said to the paralytic—

"I say to you, stand up, take your mat and go to your home." And he stood up, and immediately took the mat and went out before all of them; so that they were all amazed and glorified God, saying, "We have never seen anything like this!"

Obviously the episode is complete without the controversy in verses 5b-10. Jesus' authority to forgive sins as the Son of Man was a concern of the early church, and the forgiveness controversy was inserted into the narrative to treat the healing as a confirmation of this authority.

Even if Jesus forgave sins, he may have believed simply that he was empowered to speak on God's behalf. Viewing this as a claim to divinity is stretching things just a little.

In John's Gospel, Jesus talks about little but himself and his relationship with God. In the synoptic Gospels, however, Jesus often seems reluctant to spell out anything concerning his identity, and doesn't claim to be God or expect to be an object of worship.

An example will show the contrast between Jesus' relationship with God, and Jesus' message, in the Synoptics and John's Gospel. In Mark 10.17-18, a rich man says to Jesus, "'Good teacher, what must I do to inherit eternal life?' Jesus said to him, 'Why do you call me good? No one is good but God alone.'" Here, Jesus doesn't even want the man to call him "good," and there is no indication in Jesus' response that he equates himself with God. (We should note that this statement was an embarrassment for the church, and Matthew 19.17 changes Jesus' response to, "Why do you ask me about what is good?".)

In addition, Jesus tells the rich man that, to have eternal life, he must follow the commandments, sell all his possessions and follow him. Jesus challenges the man to give up his reliance on material things so he "will have treasure in heaven." Jesus also tells rich man to follow him, but this doesn't mean "accept me as your personal savior," or "believe in me;" it means just what it says—"follow me." Jesus tells the man to become his disciple and put God's kingdom first in his life. It should also be noted that, in Luke 10.25-28, Jesus doesn't make becoming a disciple a requirement of salvation, but says that doing "what is written in the law" is sufficient.

In John's Gospel, Jesus has a totally different message and view of himself. In response to a question from his disciple Thomas, Jesus says (John 14.6), "I am the way, and the truth, and the life. No one comes to the Father except through me." Here, Jesus doesn't talk about the commandments, but places himself at the center of things. He stresses his own intimate relationship with God and the necessity for belief in this relationship as a condition of salvation. I believe this Christ-centered view of salvation was developed by the community that produced the fourth Gospel and was not part of Jesus' message of the kingdom of God.

Before moving on, I would like to mention six factors that led Jesus' followers to exalt him as they did after his death. (1) It started with the total commitment Jesus demanded from his disciples. People who leave their families and livelihoods to follow someone have already exalted that person in some sense. (2) The fact that Jesus was rejected so vehemently by so many inevitably led his followers to choose sides and exalt him all the more. (3) Jesus clearly had some powerful religious experiences and this "outpouring of the Spirit" was passed along to his followers, who consequently venerated him because of his impact on their lives. (4) Jesus spoke with passionate feeling to a group of people who had been rejected by most of society. It is no wonder that such followers would exalt Jesus— he was truly their savior. (5) Jesus' reluctance to discuss the matter of his identity may have left the door open for the Christological free-for-all that ensued after his death. (6) There is little doubt that much of the theological speculation concerning Jesus' identity in the New Testament resulted from the resurrection experiences of his followers who, after his death, "saw" Jesus.

The Suffering Servant in Isaiah

Any discussion of Jesus' identity should mention Isaiah's suffering servant. This image may have contributed to Jesus' understanding of his ministry and view of Israel's destiny, and it certainly came to be important in the church's understanding of Jesus.

The second part of the book of Isaiah speaks of a suffering servant, and contains what have come to be known as "servant songs" describing this servant. There are four of these songs, as follows:

Isaiah 42.1-4
Isaiah 49.1-7
Isaiah 50.4-11
Isaiah 52.13-53.12

Traditionally, Christians have seen the servant songs, particularly the final song in chapters 52 and 53, as prophecies of Jesus. Christians believe that the servant songs predict Jesus' humiliation and rejection, his vicarious suffering, and his resurrection and exaltation.

However, in Isaiah 49.3, the servant is explicitly identified as Israel: "And he said to me, 'You are my servant, Israel, in whom I will be glorified.'" There are numerous other instances where this identification is explicit. For example, in Isaiah 44.21-22 God says:

Remember these things, O Jacob,
and Israel, for you are my servant;

I formed you, you are my servant;
O Israel, you will not be forgotten by me.
I have swept away your transgressions like a cloud,
and your sins like mist;
return to me, for I have redeemed you.

Isaiah is announcing Israel's vindication by its God and the destiny to which it is called as it returns from exile in Babylon. This is the theme of the second part of Isaiah (chapters 40-66). The historical context of these chapters is shown by the following verses (Isaiah 44.24a, 26b, 28):

Thus says the Lord, your Redeemer,
who formed you in the womb...
who says of Jerusalem, "It shall be inhabited,"
and of the cities of Judah,
"They shall be rebuilt,
and I will raise up their ruins"...
who says of Cyrus [the Persian king who will free Israel],
"He is my shepherd,
and he shall carry out all my purpose";
and who says of Jerusalem,
"It shall be rebuilt,"
and of the temple,
"Your foundation shall be laid."

Although the servant is often identified as Israel, some think that a historical figure is described in some of the servant songs—possibly a prophetic figure who had already died at the time the servant songs were written.

In any case, I believe Isaiah's image of the suffering servant was important for Jesus' understanding of his ministry and Israel's purpose. Jesus calls Israel to its destiny in words strikingly similar to Isaiah's: "You are the light of the world. A city built on a hill cannot be hid. No one after lighting a lamp puts it under the bushel basket, but on the lampstand, and it gives light to all in the house (Matthew 5.14-15)." The "city on a hill" is an obvious reference to Jerusalem and in this statement Jesus calls Israel to be a light to the nations.

I believe that when Jesus heard verses like Isaiah 49.5-6 he found his calling:

> And now the Lord says,
> who formed me in the womb to be his servant,
> to bring Jacob back to him,
> and that Israel might be gathered to him,
> for I am honored in the sight of the Lord,
> and my God has become my strength—
> he says,
> "It is too light a thing that you
> should be my servant
> to raise up the tribes of Jacob
> and to restore the survivors of Israel;
> I will give you as a light to the nations,
> that my salvation may reach to the end of the earth."

This makes the servant sound like an individual, but not all of Israel was taken into Babylon and not all of the exiles had been faithful. In the above verses Isaiah is probably speaking to the faithful remnant of Israel. However, I believe that, when Jesus read these words, he saw his name written between the lines. It is likely that Jesus' followers came to understand his ministry by referring to these verses because that's what Jesus did.

When Isaiah wrote, Israel had suffered under an oppressor and was about to be vindicated and called to a higher purpose. Israel was oppressed in Jesus' time also, and Jesus called it to fulfill its destiny. Israel hoped for a glorified king to crush the Romans; Jesus gave it a suffering servant instead.

4

JESUS' TEACHING

The Prophetic Nature of Jesus' Message

The prophetic nature of Jesus' message and ministry has traditionally been minimized or ignored because the church has preferred to view Jesus in much loftier terms. However, to properly understand how Jesus saw himself and his mission, we must understand his prophetic role. To do this we must first identify some of the basic features of prophetic activity in Israel. We can start with a brief summary of prophecy in Israel, and then examine the message and ministry of Jesus the prophet. I would also like to discuss the intended recipients of Jesus' message.

Prophecy in Israel:

Prophecy in Israel is a complex phenomenon that developed over a long period, and it is difficult to make generalizations about Israel's prophets. The prophets were very different in their roles in society, their backgrounds, and the nature of their activity and message. The variety of prophetic activity in Israel's early history may result from different traditions among the tribes and the assimilation of Canaanite prophetic forms by Israel.

We know of Israel's earliest prophets only through narratives that have focused primarily on their exploits in the context of Israel's history, while collections of prophecies uttered by the later prophets (those who lived after 800 BCE) were written down and transmitted in the form of books bearing their names.

Sometimes the prophets were part of the religious establishment and other times they challenged it from the outside. In either case, the greatest prophets often called for the reform of religious practices, and a redirection of attention from ritual observance to moral behavior. The message of the prophet Micah is typical of such prophets (Micah 6.6-8):

"With what shall I come before
the Lord,
and bow myself before God
on high?
Shall I come before him with
burnt offerings,
with calves a year old?
Will the Lord be pleased with
thousands of rams,
with ten thousands of rivers
of oil?
Shall I give my firstborn for my

transgression,
the fruit of my body for the sin
of my soul?"
He has told you, O mortal, what
is good;
and what does the Lord
require of you
but to do justice, and to love
kindness,
and to walk humbly with
your God?

In Amos 5.21-24, God rejects the superficial aspects of religiosity and demands righteousness with the following words:

I hate, I despise your festivals,
and I take no delight in your
solemn assemblies.
Even though you offer me your
burnt offerings and grain
offerings,
I will not accept them;
and the offerings of well-being of
your fatted animals
I will not look upon.
Take away from me the noise of your songs;
I will not listen to the melody
of your harps.
But let justice roll down like
waters,
and righteousness like an
ever-flowing stream.

With similar language, in Isaiah 1.11,15-17 God rejects reliance on ritual sacrifice and demands justice:

What to me is the multitude of

your sacrifices?
says the Lord;
I have had enough of burnt
offerings of rams
and the fat of fed beasts;
I do not delight in the blood
of bulls,
or of lambs, or of goats.
When you stretch out your hands,
I will hide my eyes from you;
even though you make many
prayers,
I will not listen;
your hands are full of blood.
Wash yourselves; make yourselves
clean;
remove the evil of your doings
from before my eyes;
cease to do evil,
learn to do good;
seek justice,
rescue the oppressed,
defend the orphan,
plead for the widow.

Israel's greatest prophets always talk about some future activity of God. Usually, they say that God is about to judge Israel for some shortcoming, and that this judgment is meant to lead Israel to repentance and a renewal of the covenant relationship. The prophetic message is based on the assumption that God's judgment is necessary to punish Israel, and only this punishment will bring about repentance.[1] The threat of judgment is usually coupled with the prospect of redemption if Israel repents and turns to God. In Isaiah 1.18-20, the choices available to Israel are given as follows:

Come now, let us argue it out,
says the Lord:
though your sins are like scarlet,
they shall be like snow;
though they are red like crimson,
they shall become like wool.
If you are willing and obedient,
you shall eat the good of the
land;
but if you refuse and rebel,
you shall be devoured by the
sword;
for the mouth of the Lord has
spoken.

The prophets generally begin their work because they have been called by God, and this call is one that cannot be resisted. Amos described God's call and his response to it in words that would be appropriate for most of the prophets (Amos 3.8):

The lion has roared;
who will not fear?
The Lord God has spoken;
who can but prophesy?

As Amos says (Amos 3.4a), "Does a lion roar in the forest, when it has no prey?" When God calls a prophet it is time for action, because God's judgment is imminent.

Significant features of prophetic activity in Israel are the great sacrifices the prophets must make, the hardships they must endure, and the controversy and opposition their message typically brings. These sacrifices and hardships are often very personal in nature and involve the acting out of the message the prophets are commanded to convey: Amos is commanded by God to marry a prostitute to illustrate Israel's unfaithfulness to God; Ezekiel is commanded to lie on his side for 390 days and to cook his food using "human dung" in order to prophesy against Jerusalem; Isaiah is commanded to walk about naked for three years "as a sign and a portent against Egypt and Ethiopia" (Isaiah 20.3).

An example of the opposition the prophets encountered is the response to Jeremiah's announcement of God's impending judgment on Jerusalem and its temple (Jeremiah 26.8-10):

And when Jeremiah had finished speaking all that the Lord had commanded him to speak to all the people, then the priests and the prophets and all the people laid hold of him, saying, "You shall die! Why have you prophesied in the name of the Lord, saying, 'This house shall be like Shiloh, and this city shall be desolate, without inhabitants'?" And all the people gathered around Jeremiah in the house of the Lord.

It isn't hard to understand why the great prophets were often very unpopular and isolated individuals. Their message was often characterized by moral indignation and predictions of doom, and for each prophet who spoke of God's judgment there was a multitude of "false prophets" who spoke words of reassurance. Consequently, the lives of the great prophets were often difficult and dangerous. Jesus' ministry was no different.

Israel's situation in Jesus' time was peculiar, insofar as prophecy was concerned. It had been centuries since a great prophet had arisen in Israel, and the times in which Jesus lived were very different from the times of Isaiah, Jeremiah and Ezekiel. One striking difference between the time of the earlier prophets and the first century involves the view of an afterlife, which was not widespread during the sixth century BCE but was widely accepted during Jesus' time. Consequently, it should not surprise us that Jesus addressed so much of his message to individuals, unlike the earlier prophets, who generally addressed Israel as a whole.

Jesus' Prophetic Ministry:

Jesus' message was essentially prophetic, and his life followed the example of the greatest prophets. He called on Israel to repent and turn to God, and threatened God's judgment on Israel if his message was ignored. Like many of the prophets, his call to proclaim God's message took precedence over everything else in his life—his family, material possessions, his work—he left all of it behind. Jesus' message was fundamentally about what God expects from his people, and the consequences to Israel of ignoring its covenant responsibilities. At the conclusion of Jesus' ministry he went to Jerusalem, entered the temple, and challenged the Jewish religious establishment, and the Roman empire, directly. This was not the approach that would have been taken by some innovative rabbi with a novel interpretation of the Torah; it was the act of a prophet willing to teach his people with his actions and his life.

One point relating to the phenomenon of prophecy in general is relevant when considering Jesus' ministry. Societies that accept prophecy typically have a traditional set of expectations about how prophets are supposed to act. Prophets that step outside these boundaries of acceptable behavior risk being rejected or having their sanity questioned.[2] If Jesus' actions and method of teaching differed from the prophetic model of his time he would have caused a lot of controversy. This seems to have been the case. Jesus forgave sins, healed the sick and the lame, challenged traditions, and he preached a message of hope to the dispossessed and judgment to the influential. He also ignored the prophetic practice of speaking in oracles and spoke on his own authority. In short, he was a unique individual who challenged traditional views and boundaries. In light of these factors, it isn't surprising that Jesus' ministry caused a series of controversies that ultimately ended with his death.

Jesus' Mission to Israel:

You might expect that, if Jesus' message was prophetic in nature, it would be delivered to Israel. This seems to be the case, as indicated by a number of verses and parables in the Gospels. The most obvious indication that Jesus directed his message and ministry to Israel is found at Matthew 10.5-6, where Jesus sends out the twelve to preach with the following instructions: "Go nowhere among the Gentiles, and enter no town of the Samaritans, but go rather to the lost sheep of the house of Israel."

Another passage that indicates Jesus directed his message to Israel is found in Mark 7.24-30. In this episode, a Phoenician woman asks Jesus to drive a demon out of her daughter. Jesus responds with the following remark (verse 27): "Let the children be fed first, for it is not fair to take the children's food and throw it to the dogs!" The woman's reply was "Sir, even the dogs under the table eat the children's crumbs." Jesus obviously liked this response because he healed her daughter, but his comment, which is really quite brutal and politically incorrect, states clearly that he believed his mission was to Israel first and foremost. Matthew 15.21-28 repeats this story and adds the explicit statement by Jesus that he "was sent only to the lost sheep of the house of Israel" (verse 24).

A mission to the Gentiles was at least implicit in Jesus' message, however. In Matthew 5.13, Jesus says, "You are the salt of the earth; but if salt has lost its taste, how can its saltiness be restored? It is no longer good for anything, but is thrown out and trampled under foot." With this statement, Jesus is calling Israel to be a guide to the nations. He is speaking of the calling that Israel has from its God and warning of his judgment if Israel doesn't repent.

Christians believe that a mission to the Gentiles is not just implicit in Jesus' message, but very explicit. After all, in

Matthew 28.19-20 the risen Christ instructs the disciples to "make disciples of all nations." However, I believe this statement, and the other such mission statements in the synoptic Gospels (for example, Luke 24.47), are developments of the early church. In any case, though, these statements tell us that the *disciples* were to minister to the Gentiles; they don't tell us that Jesus directed *his* ministry to them.

In connection with the intended recipients of Jesus' message, I would like to comment on the incident in Nazareth's synagogue where Jesus reads from Isaiah and then says that the prophecy has been fulfilled (Luke 4.16-30). Something like this could have happened, but probably not the way Luke describes it. While Jesus may have looked to Isaiah and found his calling, lifting words of the prophets out of context and treating them as a "prophecy" seems to be the province of the early church. Also, what Jesus actually says in this episode sounds too much like Luke. The thrust of Jesus' remarks is that he is to be rejected by Israel and accepted by the Gentiles. This sermonette appears to be Luke's commentary on Jesus' ministry, not something that Jesus actually said.

Jesus used the parable of the fig tree at Luke 13.6-9 to describe his mission:

> Then he told them this parable: "A man had a fig tree planted in his vineyard; and he came looking for fruit on it and found none. So he said to the gardener, 'See here! For three years I have come looking for fruit on this fig tree, and still I find none. Cut it down! Why should it be wasting the soil?' He replied, 'Sir, let it alone for one more year, until I dig around it and put manure on it. If it bears fruit next year, well and good; but if not, you can cut it down.'"

I believe this parable is an authentic description of Jesus' view of his mission, because only Jesus would refer to his ministry as spreading manure. This defiant, almost irreverent, sense of humor permeates his parables. In this parable Jesus is saying that Israel must turn to its God or face his judgment. In other words, "repent, for the kingdom of God is near."

The Kingdom of God

> The time is fulfilled, and the kingdom of God has come near; repent, and believe in the good news (Mark 1.15).

These are the first words spoken by Jesus in Mark's Gospel and they are essentially identical to the Matthew's version of Jesus' earliest teaching (see Matthew 4.17).

Most scholars agree that the kingdom of God was central to Jesus' message, but there is widespread disagreement on exactly how Jesus envisioned or what he meant by "the kingdom of God." I would like to discuss four aspects of the kingdom: eschatological, present, relational and prophetic. There will be some overlap between these, but I think this will be a useful way to examine the different dimensions of Jesus' message of the kingdom.

The eschatological kingdom:

Ever since Albert Schweitzer's "Quest of the Historical Jesus," Jesus' message of the kingdom of God has been seen by many scholars as fundamentally eschatological in nature. In other words, Jesus was declaring that the "end of the world" was near and a new age was about to dawn.

An example of a statement of the kingdom with a definite eschatological orientation is found at Luke 13.28-29:

> There will be weeping and gnashing of teeth when you see Abraham and Isaac and Jacob and all the prophets in the kingdom of God, and you yourselves thrown out. Then people will come from east and west, from north and south, and will eat in the kingdom of God.

Another example is found at Matthew 25.31-46. In these verses the Son of Man judges the nations. The righteous and the wicked are contrasted using the images of sheep and goats. In verse 34, "the king" says to the righteous, "Come, you that are blessed by my Father, inherit the kingdom prepared for you from the foundation of the world."

The imminent arrival of an eschatological event is emphasized at Matthew 24.34-35, where, after describing the events that will accompany the destruction of Jerusalem and the end of the age, Jesus says, "Truly I tell you, this generation will not pass away until all these things have taken place. Heaven and earth will pass away, but my words will not pass away." Mark 13.30-31 and Luke 21.32-33 contain identical statements. However, this statement doesn't mention the kingdom explicitly—it just says "these things" will occur during the current generation. The original statement might have been referring to something other than an eschatological end of the age.

It is interesting that, when you would most expect some mention of the kingdom in an eschatological setting, there often is none. An example is the "little apocalypse" of Mark 13. This chapter talks about the end of the age but doesn't mention the "kingdom of God." Similarly, many of the "coming of the Son of Man" statements don't mention the kingdom explicitly, although a reference to the kingdom is often placed nearby (for example, Mark 8.38, Matthew 19.28-29, Luke 17.22-30).

I believe there was an eschatological dimension to Jesus' teaching, but this aspect of Jesus' proclamation of the kingdom has been greatly overemphasized in the Gospels and by scholars. The connection between the destruction of Jerusalem and the end of the age was not a part of Jesus' original teaching, and the statement found in Mark 9.1 ("Truly I tell you, there are some standing here who will not taste death until they see that the kingdom of God has come with power.") and its parallels in Matthew and Luke originally referred to something other than "the end of the world."

I believe the statements of Jesus that speak of an imminent eschatological event are assertions of the early church, and are based on the belief that Jesus' resurrection was the beginning of the general resurrection of the dead at the end of the age. This belief is indicated by Paul's statement in 1 Corinthians 15.20-24:

> ...Christ has been raised from the dead, the first fruits of those who have died. For since death came through a human being, *the resurrection of the dead has also come* through a human being; for as all die in Adam, so all will be made alive in Christ. But each to his own order: Christ the first fruits, then at his coming those who belong to Christ. Then comes the end, when he hands over the kingdom to God the Father, after he has destroyed every ruler and every authority and power [emphasis added].

As this statement shows, the early church believed the resurrection of Jesus had initiated the new age and that Jesus would soon return from heaven to establish God's eschatological kingdom on earth.

Jesus almost certainly hoped for a heavenly kingdom on earth, but this doesn't mean he thought it was about to happen or that his proclamation of God's kingdom was fundamentally a prediction of an eschatological event. His followers came to see it that way, but I believe the Easter experience of the disciples was the basis of this belief, not the teaching of Jesus.

The present kingdom:

It is clear from Jesus' parables that he believed the kingdom of God was somehow present in his own ministry, and Jesus often spoke of the kingdom in a way that seems to have no clear relation to the end of the age. An example is the parable of the mustard seed (Matthew 13.31-32):

> The kingdom of Heaven is like a mustard seed that someone took and sowed in his field; it is the smallest of all the seeds, but when it has grown it is the greatest of shrubs and becomes a tree, so that the birds of the air come and make nests in its branches.

This parable is also found in Mark 4.30-32, Luke 13.18-19, and Thomas 20.1-4.

The image used here is a parody on the image of the kingdom of Nebuchadnezzar found in Daniel 4.10-12:

> ...there was a tree at the center of the earth,
> and its height was great.
> The tree grew great and strong,
> its top reached to heaven,
> and it was visible to the ends of
> the whole earth.
> Its foliage was beautiful,
> its fruit abundant,
> and it provided food for all.
> The animals of the field found shade under it,
> the birds of the air nested in its branches,
> and from it all living things were fed.

Jesus' parable illustrates the kingdom of God using an unexpected image. One might expect Jesus to use an exalted image like the cedars of Lebanon to describe the kingdom, but instead he uses a common mustard plant. Also, mustard is a garden pest, since it can spread rapidly and take over areas where it isn't wanted. The parable brings up the image of an inexorable power or force that is hard to resist. This image also displays a subtle sense of the wonder of things. Anyone can admire the beauty of something grand and majestic, but Jesus seems to be fond of simple images and finds the miraculous in everyday things.

The parable of the mustard seed is closely related to the parable of the leaven, and is linked to it in Matthew and Luke. This parable reads as follows (Matthew 13.33):

> The kingdom of Heaven is like yeast that a woman took and mixed in with three measures of flour until all of it was leavened.

This parable is also found at Luke 13.20-21. It is told a little differently at Thomas 96.1-2, where Jesus says that kingdom is like the woman making the bread, instead of the yeast she uses.

In this parable another everyday image is used to portray the kingdom. Here, Jesus uses leaven, which was a symbol of corruption, as an illustration of the kingdom. This is like using a Samaritan to show Jews what it means to be a neighbor. Jesus uses the unexpected, the unnoticed, the cast aside, to represent the kingdom. This is consistent with his approach to people; he spent his time searching out the lost sheep or looking for the lost coin. For Jesus, the kingdom was present in his ministry among the lowest levels of Jewish society, those considered to be corrupt and unacceptable to God.

It is difficult to see the parables of the mustard seed and the leaven as illustrations of some future cosmic event. How does someone talk about the end of the world using this kind of imagery?

These parables indicate that Jesus saw his ministry as the realization of kingdom's promise. When he sent his disciples to towns to proclaim the kingdom, they were instructed to say, "the kingdom of heaven has come near" (Matthew 10.7). He also saw his exorcisms as demonstration of the kingdom's power: "if it is by the finger of God that I cast out the demons, then the kingdom of God has come to you" (Luke 11.20).

Jesus also used parables saying that Israel has been called

to be God's servant (see Matthew 5.13, above, for an example). Such parables don't seem to indicate Jesus thought the end of history was approaching. However, they do indicate Jesus confronted Israel with a decision.

One saying of Jesus has led many to conclude that he saw the kingdom of God as a present reality, not as something that would occur in the future. This saying is found at Luke 17.20-21:

> Once Jesus was asked by the Pharisees when the kingdom of God was coming, and he answered, "The kingdom of God is not coming with things that can be observed; nor will they say, 'Look, here it is!' or 'There it is!' For, in fact, the kingdom of God is among you."

The New Revised Standard Version gives "the kingdom of God is within you" as an alternative reading. As a measure of the uncertainty surrounding the language of verse 21, the New English Bible gives the following as alternative translations in a footnote: "the kingdom of God is within you," "the kingdom of God is within your grasp," or "suddenly the kingdom of God will be among you."

It is dangerous to base too many conclusions on this single verse. This is because the Greek in Luke 17.21 is so obscure. No one is really sure what this verse is saying. However, the statement certainly seems to imply that, in some sense, the kingdom of God is present as Jesus is speaking.

One of the most difficult parables of the kingdom is found at Mark 4.26-29, and reads as follows:

> The kingdom of God is as if someone would scatter seed on the ground, and would sleep and rise night and day, and the seed would sprout and grow, he does not know how. The earth produces of itself, first the stalk, then the head, then the full grain in the head. But when the grain is ripe, at once he goes in with his sickle, because the harvest has come.

This is the only parable that is unique to Mark. It may have served as the basis for the more allegorical sowing parables in the Gospels (see Mark 4.3-8 and Matthew 13.24-30).

The references to harvest and sickle are reminiscent of Joel 3.13a, which reads, "Put in the sickle, for the harvest is ripe," and is often thought to be a metaphor for the day of judgment. The saying at Thomas 21.9 is very similar to the last verse of the above parable and to Joel 3.13a. This suggests that there is an underlying eschatological message in the parable.

It is likely, however, that this eschatological remark has been deliberately imbedded in the parable to obscure it, or to change its meaning. Jesus isn't talking about the end of the age, he is talking about sowing and reaping. Many modern readers, who live in the city, fail to realize the importance of these activities in agricultural communities, where this is the pattern of life. In Jesus' time, to reap a harvest was not some trivial matter—this was how life was sustained. After all, harvests didn't always occur, and when they did they weren't always abundant. Harvests were a time of celebration and rejoicing.

In this parable, the sower is utterly dependent for his very life on something he really doesn't understand. He doesn't question what is happening, but simply lives. When the time comes for the harvest, "at once" he gets his sickle and starts to work. This parable is an illustration of faith and living in accordance with the will of God.

This parable is also an illustration of how Jesus saw his ministry. Jesus was sowing the seed of the kingdom and the result was a harvest of those devoted to serving God without hesitation, as it is done in heaven. To go beyond this and read the end of the age into this parable is probably stretching things a little. Even if this content is there it doesn't seem to be the emphasis of the parable.

The present nature of the kingdom shouldn't be seen in isolation from its political implications. By demanding total obedience to the will of God, Jesus challenged the system of patronage during his time in uncompromising terms. Jesus' comments that his followers are free of any obligation to pay the temple tax (Matthew 17.26), and that one should not render to Caesar that which belongs to God (Mark 12.17), indicate his message of God's rule wasn't totally apolitical. Such statements are given a pacifist twist in the Gospels but they may not have been meant that way originally.

We need to consider the historical context of Jesus' proclamation of the kingdom. In Jesus' time no one's position was secure: Empires could be conquered, kings deposed, cities destroyed and their inhabitants killed or sold into slavery. In this dangerous environment simple kindness almost always lost out to territorial instincts. Jesus called upon his people to reject their dependence on the powers of this world and turn to God in repentance.

The relational kingdom:

All the discussion about the present or future reality of the kingdom should not obscure the fact that Jesus' message was not about dates and times. Jesus' message of the kingdom was about proper relationships. For Jesus, the relationship of God and man, and relationships among God's children were of first importance. This is why the bulk of Jesus' teaching is not eschatological, but ethical.

I believe Jesus' view of the kingdom is summed up nicely in the Lord's Prayer (Matthew 6.10): "Your kingdom come. Your will be done, on earth as it is in heaven." Instead of looking to the clouds of heaven, Jesus told his listeners to look to their hearts for the kingdom's promise. When they failed to heed his message, he responded with a threat of God's judgment.

The prophetic message of the kingdom:

When Jesus proclaimed that God's kingdom was imminent, I believe he was saying simply that God was about to assert his will in history, as he had done so often in the past. His message was not eschatological, but simply prophetic.

It appears that, as Jesus' ministry progressed and his call for repentance was rejected, his proclamation of the kingdom became a prophetic announcement of God's impending judgment upon Israel. An example of this is found at Matthew 11.20-24:

> Then he began to reproach the cities in which most of his deeds of power had been done, because they did not repent. "Woe to you, Chorazin! Woe to you, Bethsaida! For if the deeds of power done in you had been done in Tyre and Sidon, they would have repented long ago in sackcloth and ashes. But I tell you, on the day of judgment it will be more tolerable for Tyre and Sidon than for you. And you, Capernaum, will you be exalted to heaven? No, you will be brought down to Hades. For if the deeds of power done in you had been done in Sodom, it would have remained until this day. But I tell you that on the day of judgment it will be more tolerable for the land of Sodom than for you."

There is no use in ignoring the fact that this is a bitter statement. Jesus is telling his adopted hometown of Capernaum to go to hell, and that Sodom was a better place! We don't know what may have happened in Chorazin and Bethsaida because the Gospels tell us nothing about Jesus' activity in these towns, but apparently their reception of his message wasn't particularly gracious.

With regard to the language of the above verses, they could originally have referred to God's impending act of judgment on Israel without referring to *the* (eschatological) day of judgment.

Another indication that Jesus' message had turned to one of judgment is found at Luke 17.26-30:

> Just as it was in the days of Noah, so too it will be in the days of the Son of Man. They were eating and drinking, and marrying and being given in marriage, until the day Noah entered the ark, and the flood came and destroyed all of them. Likewise, just as it was in the days of Lot: they were eating and drinking, buying and selling, planting and building, but on the day that Lot left Sodom, it rained fire and sulfur from heaven and destroyed all of them—it will be like that on the day that the Son of Man is revealed.

While the message of impending judgment is obvious, the statement originally may not have referred to the end of the age or the coming of the Son of Man, but simply to God's impending action against Israel to punish it for rejecting Jesus' call to repentance.

When Jesus arrived at Jerusalem for the Passover during which he met his death he threatened the temple, and by extension Jerusalem, with destruction. He and his disciples apparently brought the daily routine of the temple to a screeching halt (which is exactly what the Romans did about forty years later, albeit on a more permanent basis). This action, in addition to Jesus' patently subversive message of the kingdom, led to his death at the hands of the Romans and the Jerusalem religious establishment.

I believe that, when Jesus said, "Truly I tell you, this generation will not pass away until all these things have taken place," he was talking about God's impending act of judgment on Israel, and this threat was illustrated by his actions in the temple. This was no prediction of the "end of the world," but of the events that occurred about forty years after Jesus spoke.

Like the great prophets before him, Jesus believed that God was going to punish Israel for its disobedience and that this was necessary to bring about its repentance. However, when

Jerusalem was destroyed Israel didn't embrace Jesus' message, but that of the Pharisees. Paul had hoped that the entrance of the Gentiles into the church would lead the Jews to Christ, but the opposite happened instead. In response to these events the church developed an identity crisis and the Gospels appeared to explain the situation. Jesus' hope for Israel's repentance was replaced by the belief that God's plan called for the rejection of Jesus by his people, and the subsequent rejection of Israel by God in favor of the Gentile church. The self-preservation instincts of Jews and Christians took control as they struggled to survive through the first century and their split was a painful, contentious one. What a tragic epilogue to Jesus' proclamation of God's kingdom.

Jesus and the Law

Christians view the law as something that has been superseded by the coming of Jesus Christ, who died to save us from our sins. This is indicated by the division of the Bible into an "Old Testament," or covenant, based on the law given to Israel by God at Mount Sinai, and a "New Testament," based on the atoning death of Christ, which is available to all mankind.

Christians have the words of the apostle Paul ringing in their ears whenever they think of the law. Paul's view of the law has always been controversial and hard to understand (see 2 Peter 3.16), but Christians believe Paul proclaimed the end of the law (and salvation through "works"), and the availability of salvation for all through faith in Jesus Christ.

When we look at the teaching of Jesus, however, we find something very different. In numerous episodes in the Gospels Jesus upholds the validity of the law. In addition, his earliest followers adhered to the law, including its ritual purity requirements and dietary restrictions, and appear to have found nothing in Jesus' teachings that suggested they do otherwise.

Probably the most explicit statement by Jesus concerning the status of the law is found at Matthew 5.17-18, where he says:

> Do not think that I have come to abolish the law or the prophets; I have come not to abolish but to fulfill. For truly I tell you, until heaven and earth pass away, not one letter, not one stroke of a letter, will pass from the law until all is accomplished.

The word translated as "fulfill" may also be translated as "to enforce" or "to express in its full significance." Here, Jesus says explicitly that the law is still valid and that he does not intend to do away with its requirements. Christians like to interpret Jesus' statement about "fulfilling" the law in a way that effectively negates everything else Jesus says in the above verses. They think Jesus' sacrificial death is the fulfillment of which he speaks. However, I don't think this conclusion is consistent with Jesus' teaching regarding the law in the synoptic Gospels, as the following examples should show.

Before discussing the law further, however, a couple of words regarding the nature of the law are in order. While Christians tend to see the law as the ten commandments or a longer set of legalistic rules that must be followed, it is more correct to view the law as the expression of God's covenant with his people. It is the method by which God is bound to his people in a relationship. As such, the law includes rules related to ritual purity and sacrificial observances, as well as rules that serve as guidelines for ethical conduct. We should take Jesus seriously when he says he doesn't intend to "abolish" the law, and realize that he almost certainly isn't referring just to its ethical guidelines, but to its ritual purity and sacrificial requirements as well.

Jesus doesn't try to supersede the law's requirements, but actually increases the law's demands. For example, in Mark

10.11-12, he says that "Whoever divorces his wife and marries another commits adultery against her; and if she divorces her husband and marries another, she commits adultery," even though Deuteronomy 24.1-4 allows a husband to divorce his wife. Here, Jesus uses Genesis to justify his position that, "what God has joined together, let no one separate" (Mark 10.9).

In the Sermon on the Mount Jesus seems to substantially increase the law's demands. The heading to Matthew 5.21-48 in the New Revised Standard Version says that "Jesus' Teaching Alters the Law." In these verses he seems to make the law's requirements impossible to achieve, with statements such as the following (Matthew 5.27-28):

> You have heard that it was said, "You shall not commit adultery." But I say to you that everyone who looks at a woman with lust has already committed adultery with her in his heart.

Statements such as this one have led some to believe that Jesus advocated a kind of "interim ethic" that would be in effect for the brief period before the dawn of the new age. They reason that Jesus establishes an unattainable standard that is simply unworkable as a guide for everyday living.

I believe this interpretation misses one of the most fundamental characteristics of Jesus' teaching. By increasing the law's demands, Jesus is doing what is known as "making a hedge around the Torah;" he is strengthening the law. Why? It is Jesus' intention not to invalidate or "alter" the law, but to show that it cannot be used as a source of pride or a crutch for your ego. For Jesus, what happens in your heart is the important thing, and you must turn to God in repentance. If you are to enter the kingdom you must humble yourself, not exalt yourself because of what you think are your accomplishments. The most notable illustration of this is in the parable of the Pharisee and the tax collector in Luke 18.9-14. In this parable the Pharisee exalts himself before God by saying (Luke 18.11), "God,

I thank you that I am not like other people; thieves, rogues, adulterers, or even like this tax collector." Meanwhile the tax collector will not even raise his eyes to heaven, but simply asks for forgiveness because he knows he is a sinner.

Jesus tells a story in Luke 17.7-10 that illustrates the proper attitude towards the law:

> Who among you would say to your slave who has just come in from plowing or tending sheep in the field, "Come here at once and take your place at the table"? Would you not rather say to him, "Prepare supper for me, put on your apron and serve me while I eat and drink; later you may eat and drink"? Do you thank the slave for doing what was commanded? So you also, when you have done all that you were ordered to do, say, "We are worthless slaves; we have done only what we ought to have done!"

In this story, there is no room for pride in one's accomplishments. The purpose of serving God is to serve, not to exalt oneself.

An important episode for understanding Jesus' treatment of the law is Mark 7.1-23. In this episode some of Jesus' disciples are accused of breaking the law by eating with unwashed hands. Jesus responds to this accusation with the following words (Mark 7.9-13):

> You have a fine way of rejecting the commandment of God in order to keep your tradition! For Moses said, "Honor your father and your mother"; and "Whoever speaks evil of father or mother must surely die." But you say that if anyone tells father or mother, "Whatever support you might have had from me is Corban" (that is, an offering to God)—then you no longer permit doing anything for a father or mother, thus making void the word of God through your tradition that you have handed on. And you do many things like this.

As indicated by these remarks, the Pharisees tended to be flexible in their understanding of the law. They created a substantial "tradition of the elders" to apply and interpret it. Jesus criticizes this tradition when it goes against the clear meaning of the law. The implication of Jesus' comments is that he has no interest in "making void" the law. We have already seen that Jesus increased the law's demands, and from this episode it appears that he did not approve of attempts to lessen them.

It should also be noted that Mark's comment in Mark 7.19, "Thus he declared all foods clean," is his own interpretation and is not necessarily the meaning of Jesus' words in Mark 7.15—"there is nothing outside a person that by going in can defile, but the things that come out are what defile." It seems unlikely that the law's dietary restrictions would have been such a divisive issue in the early church if Jesus had decisively spoken out against them.

Another episode involving the law, at Mark 2.23-28, concerns the observance of the sabbath. Here, Jesus' disciples are criticized by the Pharisees for plucking heads of grain on the sabbath and eating them. The Pharisees ask Jesus why his disciples are "doing what is not lawful on the sabbath" (Mark 2.24). Jesus responds by saying (Mark 2.27-28), "The sabbath was made for humankind, and not humankind for the sabbath; so the Son of Man is lord even of the sabbath."

In both of the above episodes Jesus takes issue with the legalistic approach of the Pharisees. His intention is not to invalidate the law, but to put it in the proper context. For Jesus, the law is a matter of the heart, not one of blindly following rules. It should also be noted that in these episodes Jesus is not accused of breaking the law—his disciples are. Also, in both episodes Jesus uses scripture as the basis for his position. These factors further indicate that Jesus had no interest in doing away with the law.

An indication of the importance of the law for Jesus is the discussion he has with a lawyer in Luke 10.25-28:

Just then a lawyer stood up to test Jesus. "Teacher," he said, "what must I do to inherit eternal life?" He said to him, "What is written in the law? What do you read there?" He answered, "You shall love the Lord your God with all your heart, and with all your soul, and with all your strength, and with all your mind; and your neighbor as yourself." And he said to him, "You have given the right answer; do this, and you will live."

Christians like to use the harmonizing approach to tap dance around Jesus' comments above regarding the law. Harmonizers often assert that Jesus tailors his teaching for his listeners, and will tell different people different things, depending on the circumstances. Thus, their reasoning goes, sometimes Jesus will tell someone to rely on the law for their salvation, and other times he will stress the need for faith in his divine nature and mission, and his sacrificial death. Consequently, the harmonizing approach finds no contradiction between these two radically different views of salvation. However, I believe we should take Jesus' above comments at face value, and recognize that they are probably closer to what he actually taught than the kind of salvation requirements you find in John's Gospel and the Last Supper narratives of the Synoptics. This is particularly true since these comments are consistent with numerous statements in the synoptic Gospels that stress the law's importance.

The above exchange is very similar to another, which is found in Luke 18.18-23, Matthew 19.16-22 and Mark 10.17-22. In the conversation recorded in these verses, Jesus is asked what must be done to have eternal life. His response in Matthew 19.17 is, "if you wish to enter into life, keep the commandments." He then lists a few, and then adds the requirement that the questioner should, "go, sell your possessions, and give the money to the poor, and you will have treasure in heaven;

then come, follow me" (Matthew 19.21). In this episode, Jesus again stresses the importance of keeping the commandments. He also adds the requirement to sell your possessions. This was obviously a requirement of becoming Jesus' disciple, and it was one that the rich man was unwilling to meet.

Immediately after stressing the importance of the commandments and selling your possessions, Jesus' shocked disciples ask, "Then who can be saved?" He responds by saying that, "For mortals it is impossible, but for God all things are possible" (Matthew 19.25-26). Here, immediately after he talks about the necessity of keeping the law, Jesus says that you can be saved only through the grace of God, and not through anything you have done. By doing this, Jesus once again defeats the expectations of those who hope to be vindicated by their adherence to the law, rather than reliance on God's mercy.

In Matthew 22.34-40, a lawyer asks Jesus which is the greatest commandment. Jesus responds by saying (37-40):

"You shall love the Lord your God with all your heart, and with all your soul, and with all your mind." This is the greatest and first commandment. And a second is like it: "You shall love your neighbor as yourself." On these two commandments hang all the law and the prophets.

Some take this to mean that Jesus is minimizing the importance of the law's requirements. However, Jesus is once again simply trying to place the demands of the law in the proper context, not trying to overthrow the law by saying that love of God and neighbor forms its basis.

In the 23rd chapter of Matthew Jesus says (Matthew 23.2-3): "The scribes and the Pharisees sit on Moses' seat; therefore, do whatever they teach you and follow it; but do not do as they do, for they do not practice what they teach." Clearly, the law is not being overturned here just because the Pharisees don't observe it. Then, in Matthew 23.24, Jesus says of the Pharisees: "You blind guides! You strain out a gnat but swallow a camel!" Here Jesus warns against excessive legalism with regard to the law. This is consistent with his view that the law is a matter of the heart, not a matter of following rules.

One verse some see as an indication that Jesus' life and ministry invalidated the law is Luke 16.16, where Jesus says, "The law and the prophets were in effect until John came; since then the good news of the kingdom of God is proclaimed, and everyone tries to enter it by force." This statement seems to suggest that the law no longer applies. However, in the very next verse Jesus says: "But it is easier for heaven and earth to pass away, than for one stroke of a letter in the law to be dropped." In addition, Matthew has very different wording for this statement. In Matthew 11.13 the verse reads, "For all the prophets and the law prophesied until John came." Clearly, these verses don't support the conclusion that Jesus preached the "end of the law."

As the above verses show, Jesus did not invalidate the law, or seek to replace it, but upheld it and referred to it constantly. He didn't see the law as a matter of blindly following rules, but used it as a guide for the heart, so that one could enter into the kingdom of God humbly, as a child that has been reborn. Jesus railed against the hypocrisy, superficiality and legalism of his time, and called upon Israel to turn to its God with humility and a penitent spirit.

Jesus' position with regard to the Jewish purity requirements seems to have paralleled his view of other elements of the law. For Jesus, compliance with the law's ethical requirements didn't vindicate one before God, but was the result of reliance on God's mercy. Similarly, compliance with the purity laws didn't make one pure, but was simply an affirmation of one's commitment to live in accordance with God's will; it was an outgrowth or result of inner purity.

Although Jesus did not reject the law, his teaching must

have distressed those of his Jewish listeners who thought God vindicated the righteous, and that the law could legitimately be used as a basis for the righteousness that is acceptable to God. Implicit in the teaching of Jesus was the disturbing message that even those who did not keep the law were acceptable. Additionally, Jesus' novel approach to the purity laws had to be unsettling to many Jews. It is likely that certain elements of Jewish society, particularly the lower economic classes (in other words, most of the people) and the social outcasts, welcomed Jesus' message while the more prominent members of society found it very threatening.

As the early church grew, this disturbing element of Jesus' teaching, combined with the church's exaltation of a Messiah that had been crucified as a criminal (and thus "accursed" by the law), caused the Gospel to be rejected by the Jewish people, while it was embraced by the Gentiles. The large number of Gentiles in the church made adherence to the law a burning issue. Paul believed the Gentile converts should not be held to the law and his view eventually prevailed. However, from Paul's letters we know that his position met with fierce resistance from the original followers of Jesus and their leaders, particularly James, the brother of Jesus, and Peter.

It might be argued that Paul carried Jesus' teaching to its logical conclusion by insisting that faith, not "works," leads to salvation. However, Jesus taught that "all things are possible with God," while Paul taught that you must have faith in Jesus' atoning death and his resurrection. In addition, Jesus did not address the issue of Gentiles and the law since he appears to have confined his ministry to the Jewish people.

Paul's view that Gentile converts should not be held to the law hastened the split between the Jewish and Gentile Christians, since the former could not remain faithful to the law while associating freely with Gentiles who were not. This tended to drive the Jewish Christians out of the church. Under these circumstances it is no surprise that Christianity became a Gentile religion.

As a note regarding the place of the law in early Christianity, we should consider the traditions in the early church stating that, at the day of judgment, people would be judged based on their "works," not their faith. For example, in Revelation 20.11-12, we find the following description of the judgment day:

> Then I saw a great white throne and the one who sat on it; the earth and the heaven fled from his presence, and no place was found for them. And I saw the dead, great and small, standing before the throne, and books were opened. Also another book was opened, the book of life. And *the dead were judged according to their works*, as recorded in the books [emphasis added].

Similarly, in the account of the judgment found at Matthew 25.31-46, the sheep are the righteous who inherit the kingdom based on their actions, while the goats are those who turned their backs on the needy. The view that Christians are saved purely through faith was also challenged in the Epistle of James, which says that, "faith by itself, if it has no works, is dead" (James 2.17).

It would appear that both the views of Paul and his opponents had some basis in the teachings of Jesus, but Paul carried the day in the Gentile church.

While on the subject of the law, we should address the issue of Jesus' "sacrificial" death, since this has traditionally been seen as an important aspect of Jesus' view of his relationship to the law. Jesus' followers came to see his death as a sacrificial, atoning one. This understanding of Jesus' death is one of the most striking examples of how Jesus' followers came to understand his life using images and practices found in the Hebrew Bible.

We might compare the sacrificial death of Jesus to the offering found in Leviticus 14.1-7, which gives the first part of the sacrifice necessary for the cleansing of a leper. It involves the use of two birds. In this ritual a priest wrings off the head of one bird and drains its blood into a bowl. He then dips the second bird into the blood and sprinkles the person offering the sacrifice with some of the blood. The second bird is then released by the priest. This ritual death and subsequent redemption or cleansing, and the identification of the individual with the sacrificial animals, is common in the sacrifices of the Hebrew Bible.

The traditional Christian understanding of Jesus' death is similar to this type of sacrifice. The person offering the above sacrifice is cleansed by his ritual identification with the second bird, which is "washed in the blood" of its slain counterpart and then released. Similarly, a follower of Jesus is saved by participating in his death and subsequent resurrection. There are such parallels between the understanding of Jesus' death and the other sacrifices in the Torah. It should also be pointed out that the traditional view of Jesus as "sinless" is based on the requirements in Leviticus that sacrificial animals be without blemish.

There are a couple of significant differences between the Hebrew Bible sacrifices and the Christian variety that should be noted. First, Christianity is based on a human sacrifice, not the sacrifice of an animal. This doesn't seem to cause many people a problem. Perhaps the theological understanding of Jesus' death mitigates this element of human sacrifice somewhat. This is because, unlike the Jewish sacrifice, which is performed by a ritually clean priest on behalf of a sinful human, the Christian sacrifice is offered by a holy God and his sacrifice is killed by unclean Gentiles. This is a dramatic departure from the traditional sacrifices of the Hebrew Bible.

Based on his teaching in the synoptic Gospels, it doesn't appear that Jesus saw his death as some kind of universal, one-time atonement for mankind's sins. The most explicit statements by Jesus in these Gospels regarding a sacrificial death are found in the Last Supper narratives, which have been influenced by the theological reflection and ritual life of the early church. I don't think the words attributed to Jesus at the Last Supper were actually spoken by him; they are later interpretations of his ministry. Surely, Jesus had a last meal with his disciples before the cleansing of the temple and spoke of his impending death at this time. He almost certainly believed his death would be shared by some of his disciples and told them to be prepared for this. In fact, I believe he told them this before he ever came to Jerusalem and this is why many of them had already left him. When Jesus spoke of his disciples sharing his baptism (Mark 10.38), I think he was preparing them for the possibility that they might die with him and later be raised at the resurrection, but not that they would share in his death and resurrection through some kind of substitutionary atonement.

When Jesus spoke of giving his life as a "ransom for many" (Mark 10.45), I believe he was referring to the fact that he had forsaken everything and devoted his life to his ministry. He may also have meant that, by giving himself up to be killed, he would eliminate the threat of action against his followers. We should remember that Pilate was removed from his office partly because of a brutal action he took against a religious faction soon after Jesus' death.

I don't see any evidence in Jesus' parables that he saw his death as the basis for some kind of new covenant that would supersede the "Old Testament." An atoning, sacrificial death just isn't there. I believe Jesus saw his death as the culmination of his ministry, as the final teaching he had to offer. He didn't seek to replace the covenant relationship of God with his people, but to renew it. He probably saw his death, and his life, as having redemptive meaning in the sense that, through his ministry, God was reaching out to his people. However, I don't believe Jesus saw his death as a sacrificial one along the patterns of Leviticus or as an atonement for mankind's sin.

Jesus may not have seen his death as an atoning sacrifice, but it seems logical that his followers would interpret his ministry in this way. The traditional sacrifices of the Hebrew Bible provided a way to approach God, but also protected those who offered the sacrifices from God's holiness. This holiness was seen as a destructive force that would kill anyone who did not observe the necessary precautions for entering into God's presence. Jesus challenged this view by saying that God's holiness is not just a destructive force, but a redemptive power that reaches out and embraces that which is unholy; God's nature is one of forgiveness and love. Jesus taught that continual ritual maneuvers are not necessary to enter into the presence of God, but only compassion, mercy and faithfulness. He also emphasized the natural corollary of this: The presence and power of God is most fully revealed in human affairs when simple kindness serves as the basis for action. In this sense, the teaching of Jesus certainly could be said to have completed or "fulfilled" the law.

Jesus and Money

The message of Jesus in the Gospels regarding money is consistent and simple: it is a hindrance to entering the kingdom of God. All three of the synoptic Gospels contain the story of the man who refused to follow Jesus because he wouldn't part with his possessions, along with Jesus' statement that, "It is easier for a camel to go through the eye of a needle than for someone who is rich to enter the kingdom of God" (Mark 10.25).

Luke's Gospel contains a number of sayings and parables that warn about the dangers of wealth. In Luke 14.33, Jesus actually says to a crowd of people, "none of you can become my disciple if you do not give up all your possessions." In Luke 16.19-31, Jesus tells the story of the rich man and Lazarus, the poor man who lived at the rich man's gate. Lazarus was taken by the angels to be with Abraham while the rich man went to hell. A similar message is given in the parable of the rich fool at Luke 12.16-21, where a rich man plans to "eat, drink and be merry" but dies that very night. In Luke 16.13, we find Jesus saying, "You cannot serve God and wealth."

The Sermon on the Mount contains a number of similar sayings. Jesus tells his listeners not to run after worldly things because, "where your treasure is, there your heart will be also" (Matthew 6.21).

Thus, the synoptic Gospels consistently show Jesus warning against becoming attached to wealth, since this attachment is a distraction from the one thing that is important—entering the kingdom.

We shouldn't overlook the potential for Jesus' condemnation of wealth to cause controversy and polarize his listeners along economic lines. We often hear about the sublimity of the beatitudes, but the woes that accompany them in Luke don't get much press. In Luke 6.24-25, Jesus says:

> But woe to you who are rich,
> for you have received your consolation.
> Woe to you who are full now,
> for you will be hungry.
> Woe to you who are
> laughing now,
> for you will mourn and weep.

Also, Jesus condemned what were probably prosperous Galilean towns that rejected his message, and blasted Pharisees who took advantage of their position for personal gain. His message that roles are reversed in the kingdom could not have endeared him to the more prosperous of his listeners. By deliberately targeting his message to the downtrodden and the destitute, Jesus could easily have isolated himself from the more established elements of Jewish society.

We should keep in mind that, during Jesus' day, most

people were poor, and there was little in the way of a middle class. Additionally, in rural Galilee money could have been seen as an instrument of oppression that allowed the large, powerful estates of the nobility to dominant the peasants. These peasants had traditionally used barter within the context of their small communities, and achieved little more than a subsistence level of production even in good years. The use of money and extensive export of the region's produce contributed to the impoverishment of the poorer members of Jewish society. Jesus seems to have directed his message to the masses of the people who were, as he saw it, oppressed by the more powerful members of society. For Jesus, this was not an economic issue, but a moral one.

Jesus and Family

It is not an easy thing for many Christians to accept, but the consistent testimony of the Gospels is that Jesus regarded family ties as a hindrance to discipleship. Probably the most brutally difficult statement Jesus makes in all of the Gospels is found at Luke 14.26:

> Whoever comes to me and does not hate father and mother, wife and children, brothers and sisters, yes, and even life itself, cannot be my disciple.

This drastic, uncompromising rejection of family relationships is consistent with the sense of urgency that Jesus' obviously felt regarding his mission. This sense of urgency doesn't necessarily imply an eschatological outlook, but could just as easily have resulted from the prophetic nature of Jesus ministry.

Jesus clearly believed his message was a divisive one, as indicated by the following statement at Luke 12.51-53:

Do you think that I have come to bring peace to the earth? No, I tell you, but rather division! From now on five in one household will be divided, three against two and two against three; they shall be divided:

> father against son
> and son against father,
> mother against daughter
> and daughter against mother,
> mother-in-law against her
> daughter-in-law
> and daughter-in-law against
> mother-in-law.

This verse echoes Micah 7.6, which describes a similar inter-generational conflict.

A few incidents in the Gospels suggest that division was a fact of Jesus' family life. In Mark 3.31-35 we find the following episode:

> Then his mother and his brothers came; and standing outside, they sent to him and called him. A crowd was sitting around him; and they said to him, "Your mother and your brothers and sisters are outside, asking for you." And he replied, "Who are my mother and my brothers?" And looking at those who sat around him, he said, "Here are my mother and my brothers! Whoever does the will of God is my brother and sister and mother."

This episode is reproduced at Matthew 12.46-50 and Luke 8.19-21, and both versions are substantially identical to Mark's.

Similarly, at Luke 11.27-28, we find the following episode:

> While he was saying this, a woman in the crowd raised her voice and said to him, "Blessed is the womb that bore you

and the breasts that nursed you!" But he said, "Blessed rather are those who hear the word of God and obey it."

When a would-be follower tells Jesus he must first bury his father, Jesus replies, "Let the dead bury their own dead; but as for you, go and proclaim the kingdom of God" (Luke 9.60). It isn't likely that these verses indicate a happy situation at home, but they do indicate that Jesus practiced what he preached and didn't ask things of his disciples he was unwilling to do himself. The shocking nature of this last statement should not be missed—burying one's father was seen as an important obligation in Jewish society. Jesus' statement shows the uncompromising commitment he has to his message and ministry.

In an episode recorded in Mark 12.18-27, Matthew 22.23-33, and Luke 20.27-38, some Sadducees tell Jesus the story of the woman who married seven brothers in succession, then died. They ask whose wife she would be in heaven. In Luke 20.34-36 Jesus tells them:

Those who belong to this age marry and are given in marriage; but those who are considered worthy of a place in that age and in the resurrection of the dead neither marry nor are given in marriage. Indeed they cannot die anymore, because they are like angels and are children of God, being children of the resurrection.

For Jesus, the kingdom of God was all that mattered, and family ties had lost all of their relevance.

In Luke 9.61-62 another would-be disciple says to Jesus, "I will follow you, Lord; but let me first say farewell to those at my home." Jesus said to him, "No one who puts a hand to the plow and looks back is fit for the kingdom of God."

This episode obviously parallels the call of Elisha by Elijah at 1 Kings 19.19-21:

So [Elijah]...found Elisha..., who was plowing. Elisha passed by him and threw his mantle over him. [Elisha] left the oxen, ran after Elijah, and said, "Let me kiss my father and my mother, and then I will follow you." Then Elijah said to him, "Go back again; for what have I done to you?" [Elisha] returned...then...followed Elijah, and became his servant.

Elijah gives Elisha permission (in an obscure verse) to return home and say good-bye to his parents, while Jesus won't even allow a potential follower to bury his own father! Family ties for Jesus have lost all of their significance. Probably no other aspect of Jesus' teaching brings out the urgency of his mission and his message of the kingdom.

I don't believe Jesus expected everyone who heard his voice to abandon their families and follow him. His prohibition of divorce (Mark 10.2-10) would make little sense if he had insisted that everyone should simply disregard their family obligations. However, I believe he expected his disciples to leave their families as well as their possessions and occupations. Jesus recognized that his view of family ties wasn't for everyone, as his comment, "Not everyone can accept this teaching," would indicate (Matthew 19.11).

The Parables

The synoptic Gospels tell us that Jesus used parables as a method of teaching. In fact, it has been estimated that about one third of all Jesus' teaching is comprised of parables. The word "parable" comes from the Greek word "parabole," which means to compare one thing with another, or to set one thing beside, or parallel with, something else. The Hebrew word underlying the Greek parabole is "mashal," which comes from an Akkadian root "masalu," meaning "to compare." The word mashal has acquired a rather broad meaning; it can mean a proverb, riddle or even verse, but is most commonly used in the sense of a "story parable," a story in which some type of comparison is made.[3]

Many of Jesus' parables are stories or images that compare the kingdom of God to something. Others deal with issues such as prayer and forgiveness. All use concrete, everyday images that would be familiar to Jesus' listeners.

Although they use familiar images from everyday life, the parables have often puzzled those who encounter them. Many have interpreted the parables in an involved allegorical manner that often strays from the intended message. Although some parables are allegorical in nature to some extent, most are simply comparisons where, for example, a mustard tree is a mustard tree, not an allegorical representation of something else. In short, most of the parables use comparison, not allegory. The distinction may be a fine one at times but it is one that should be kept in mind.

The number of parables you find in the Gospels depends on what you call a parable. About forty are commonly identified, but this figure doesn't include parabolic sayings such as "you are the salt of the earth." Most of the parables traditionally identified as such tend to be stories or images constructed with multiple sentences, rather than single verses.

The synoptic Gospels provide a strange rationale for Jesus' use of parables. In Mark 4.10-13 we find Jesus giving the following reason for his parabolic teaching:

> When he was alone, those who were around him along with the twelve asked him about the parables. And he said to them, "To you has been given the secret of the kingdom of God, but for those outside, everything comes in parables; in order that
> > they may indeed look, but not perceive
> > and may indeed listen, but not understand;
> > so that they may not turn again and be forgiven."

This justification for the use of parables is paralleled by Matthew 13.13 and Luke 8.10.

Jesus is obviously not "alone" when he says these things in Mark's Gospel; he is with his closest disciples. Jesus says that the disciples are privileged to get an explanation of his parables, while the crowds that gather around him are meant to be confused. In other words, Mark is saying that Jesus used parables to hide the "secret" of the kingdom of God from his listeners! Apparently, Mark thought that the parables were difficult to understand so he could live with this idea. This rationale is a part of Mark's explanation for the rejection of Jesus by the Jewish people, which is an important theme in his Gospel, but it isn't the reason Jesus used parables. Jesus used parables to succinctly illustrate a point that might otherwise be turned into a dry philosophical or technical discourse; the purpose of Jesus' parabolic instruction was to communicate a message, not to obscure one.

Since the parables of Jesus are an integral part of his teaching, I would like to go through some of the more important ones that have not been dealt with elsewhere in this book to see what light they shed on Jesus' life and ministry. I will identify each parable, give a brief analysis of its meaning, and comment on whether the parable appears to have originated with Jesus.

Before going through the parables in detail, however, I would like to make a couple of points regarding my approach and findings. First, I believe that parables with a strong allegorical content or structure tend not to be the original versions of such parables. Jesus' parables weren't detailed allegories that contain a hidden meaning needing explanation, but simple illustrations designed to make a point.

Next, Jesus doesn't usually appear in his parables. If parables were a substantial part of Jesus' teaching, and the parables tend to talk about something other than Jesus, it is hard to conclude that Jesus talked about himself a lot, or that he saw himself playing some kind of essential, central role in the kingdom of God. In his parables, Jesus usually talks about the kingdom of God, forgiveness, or his ministry, but not about himself.

The Parable of the Great Dinner

This parable is found at Luke 14.16-24, Matthew 22.2-10 and Thomas 64.1-12. It is a good example of how a parable with a simple message is converted into an allegory.

In Luke 14.16-24, Jesus tells the parable this way:

Someone gave a great dinner and invited many. At the time for the dinner he sent his slave to say to those who had been invited, "Come; for everything is ready now." But they all alike began to make excuses. The first said to him, "I have bought a piece of land, and I must go out and see it; please accept my regrets." Another said, "I have bought five yoke of oxen, and I am going to try them out; please accept my regrets." Another said, "I have just been married, and therefore I cannot come." So the slave returned and reported this to his master. Then the owner of the house became angry and said to his slave, "Go out at once into the streets and lanes of the town and bring in the poor, the crippled, the blind, and the lame." And the slave said, "Sir, what you ordered has been done, and there is still room." Then the master said to the slave, "Go out into the roads and lanes, and compel people to come in, so that my house may be filled. For I tell you, none of those who were invited will taste my dinner."

In Matthew 22.2-10, the parable is told like this:

The kingdom of heaven may be compared to a king who gave a wedding banquet for his son. He sent his slaves to call those who had been invited to the wedding banquet, but they would not come. Again he sent other slaves, saying, "Tell those who have been invited: Look, I have prepared my dinner, my oxen and my fat calves have been slaughtered, and everything is ready; come to the wedding banquet." But they made light of it and went away, one to his farm, another to his business, while the rest seized his slaves, mistreated them, and killed them. The king was enraged. He sent his troops, destroyed those murderers, and burned their city. Then he said to his slaves, "The wedding is ready, but those invited were not worthy. Go therefore into the main streets, and invite everyone you find to the wedding banquet." Those slaves went out into the streets and gathered all whom they found, both good and bad; so the wedding hall was filled with guests.

The version of this parable found at Thomas 64.1-12 is closer to Luke's.

In Luke, this parable simply shows that many people don't enter the kingdom because they are too busy with their everyday affairs. Those who actually enter the kingdom aren't preoccupied with temporal matters. This is consistent with Jesus' call to forsake wealth, status, family ties and all other allegiances so that one may enter the kingdom.

Matthew has taken this parable and converted it into an allegorical representation of the rejection of Jesus by the Jewish people, the persecution of the early church, and God's subsequent judgment on Israel, complete with an apparent reference to the destruction of Jerusalem in 70 CE. A simple illustration of the kingdom's importance has been transformed into an allegory with a very different meaning. Matthew completes the parable with the addition of verses 11-14, in which he provides his commentary on the low moral standards in his congregation.

This parable is a good example of how the original meaning of a saying of Jesus could get changed to suit the theological interests of an evangelist.

Now, it is possible that Jesus told this parable more than once, and he is responsible for both versions given above. However, given the close similarities between the two, it is more likely that the same basic parable made it into two different Gospels, but was changed to suit the interests of the respective evangelists.

The Parable of the Talents

Here we have another example of turning parables into allegories, only this time Luke is responsible for the changes. Matthew 25.14-30 records this parable as follows:

> For it is as if a man, going on a journey, summoned his slaves and entrusted his property to them; to one he gave five talents, to another two, to another one, to each according to his ability. Then he went away. The one who had received the five talents went off and once and traded with them, and made five more talents. In the same way, the one who had the two talents made two more talents. But the one who had received the one talent went off and dug a hole in the ground and hid his master's money. After a long time the master of those slaves came and settled accounts with them. Then the one who had received the five talents came forward, bringing five more talents, saying, "Master, you handed over to me five talents; see, I have made five more talents." His master said to him, "Well done, good and trustworthy slave; you have been trustworthy in a few things, I will put you in charge of many things; enter into the joy of your master." And the one with the two talents also came forward, saying, "Master, you handed over to me two talents; see, I have made two more talents." His master said to him, "Well done, good and trustworthy slave; you have been trustworthy in a few things, I will put you in charge of many things; enter into the joy of your master." Then the one who had received the one talent also came forward, saying, "Master, I knew that you were a harsh man, reaping where you did not sow, and gathering

where you did not scatter seed; so I was afraid, and I went and hid your talent in the ground. Here you have what is yours." But his master replied, "You wicked and lazy slave! You knew, did you, that I reap where I did not sow, and gather where I did not scatter? Then you ought to have invested my money with the bankers, and on my return I would have received what was my own with interest. So take the talent from him, and give it to the one with the ten talents. For to all those who have, more will be given, and they will have an abundance; but from those who have nothing, even what they have will be taken away. As for this worthless slave, throw him into the outer darkness, where there will be weeping and gnashing of teeth."

Luke 19.12-27, however, records the parable a little differently:

So he said, "A nobleman went to a distant country to get royal power for himself and then return. He summoned ten of his slaves, and gave them ten pounds, and said to them, 'Do business with these until I come back.' But the citizens of his country hated him and sent a delegation after him, saying, 'We do not want this man to rule over us.' When he returned, having received royal power, he ordered these slaves, to whom he had given the money, to be summoned so that he might find out what they had gained by trading. The first came forward and said, 'Lord, your pound has made ten more pounds.' He said to him, 'Well done, good slave! Because you have been trustworthy in a very small thing, take charge of ten cities.' Then the second came, saying, 'Lord, your pound has made five pounds.' He said to him, 'And you, rule over five cities.' Then the other came, saying, 'Lord, here is your pound. I wrapped it up in a piece of cloth, for I was afraid of you, because you are harsh man; you take what you did not deposit, and reap what you did not sow.' He said to him, 'I will judge you by your own words, you wicked slave! You knew, did you, that I was a harsh man, taking what I did not deposit and reaping what I did not sow? Why then did you not put my money into the bank? Then when I returned, I could have collected it with interest.' He said to the by-standers, 'Take the pound from him and give it to the one who has ten pounds.' (And they said to him, 'Lord, he has ten pounds!') 'I tell you, to all those who have, more will be given; but from those who have nothing, even what they have will be taken away. But as for these enemies of mine who did not want me to be king over them—bring them here and slaughter them in my presence.'"

The first thing in Matthew's version that would have struck Jesus' listeners is the tremendous amount of money entrusted to the servants in the parable. A talent was the equivalent of about fifteen years' wages for a common laborer in Jesus' time. Thus, each of the servants has been put in charge of a considerable fortune and, as the parable shows, the stakes involved are high.

The message of this parable is very simple: Jesus is calling on people to a make a bold decision and take action. His proclamation of the kingdom is not for the timid or the faithless, but for those who are willing to acknowledge God's grace by acting in accordance with his will.

There is no need to look for particular social groups in this parable, such as the scribes, Pharisees or Jews. The parable isn't blaming anyone in particular; it is simply attacking an attitude of faithlessness and promising a reward to those who have the courage to act.

Luke has turned this parable into an allegory designed to explain the delay of the second coming of Christ; the parable is told because the disciples, "supposed that the kingdom of God was to appear immediately" (Luke 19.11). It is complete with a prediction of God's judgment on Israel. This parable says a lot about Luke's theology and warrants a careful reading, but the version of the parable he gives us has been changed totally from its original meaning.

The Parable of the Weeds Among the Wheat

This parable is found at Matthew 13.24-30:

> The kingdom of heaven may be compared to someone who sowed good seed in his field; but while everybody was asleep, an enemy came and sowed weeds among the wheat, and then went away. So when the plants came up and bore grain, then the weeds appeared as well. And the slaves of the house-holder came and said to him, "Master, did you not sow good seed in your field? Where, then, did these weeds come from?" He answered, "An enemy has done this." The slaves said to him, "Then do you want us to go and gather them?" But he replied, "No; for in gathering the weeds you would uproot the wheat along with them. Let both of them grow together until the harvest; and at harvest time I will tell the reapers, 'Collect the weeds first and bind them in bundles to be burned, but gather the wheat into my barn."

This parable is also found at Thomas 57.1-4, but in no other canonical Gospel. Matthew 13.36-43 provides a detailed explanation for this parable.

I don't believe this parable goes back to Jesus. It appears to be an allegorical reworking of the sowing parable at Mark 4.26-29, which was obscure enough to invite further development. The detailed allegorical interpretation given for the parable was created by the early church; Jesus didn't need to "explain" his parables like this because his listeners couldn't understand what he was saying. Someone living in Galilee would probably have more familiarity with agriculture than the parable indicates—the surprise at the appearance of weeds in a field is something only a city-dweller would have. Additionally, doesn't it seem odd that the master did the sowing instead of the servants? Isn't this forcing the allegory a little too much? The details don't add up, the allegorical nature of the parable makes it suspicious, and the explanation given fits the situation of the early church too well for the parable to be original with Jesus.

The Parables of the Hidden Treasure and the Pearl

These parables are found together in Matthew 13.44-46:

The kingdom of heaven is like treasure hidden in a field, which someone found and hid; then in his joy he goes and sells all he has and buys that field.

Again, the kingdom of heaven is like a merchant in search of fine pearls; on finding one pearl of great value, he went and sold all he had and bought it.

These parables are not found in any of the other synoptic Gospels, but a version of the parable of the buried treasure is found at Thomas 109.1-3, and the parable of the pearl is found at Thomas 76.1-2. The versions in Thomas aren't significantly different from Matthew's.

In these two very similar parables Jesus emphasizes how admission into the kingdom demands singlemindedness, sacrifice and total devotion to God. They illustrate Jesus' belief that allegiances to anything other than the kingdom are irrelevant. The kingdom obviously has its reward, though, and the image of joy upon discovering buried treasure is a potent one. It must have been particularly so for Jesus' audience, many of whom had little or nothing in the way of possessions. It should also be noted that the kingdom in these parables is not a product of doing something. It is its own reward and is simply "found," not earned.

We might ask if these two parables, which appear to be so similar in meaning, talk about the kingdom in a present or future sense. They seem to suggest neither. Instead, they deal with the kind of attitude and commitment that is needed to enter the kingdom. The primary issue in the parables is the response of the individuals to a wonderful event that occurs in their lives.

It is often noted that the man who finds the hidden treasure doesn't have the highest moral standards, since he doesn't tell the owner of the property about the treasure. The man may not be a shining example of moral virtue but he isn't stupid either. Given that Jesus' listeners were often "the sinners" and not the righteous, it shouldn't surprise us that the characters in his parables are sometimes less than perfect. With regard to the man's moral standards, this parable is similar to the parable of the dishonest manager, who isn't perfect, but is smart enough to know what to do when faced with a decision. We should also give the man in this parable credit for not simply taking the treasure for himself without buying the property.

The Parable of the Dragnet

The only canonical source for this parable is Matthew 13.47-48:

> Again, the kingdom of heaven is like a net that was thrown into the sea and caught fish of every kind; when it was full, they drew it ashore, sat down, and put the good into baskets but threw out the bad.

Matthew's interpretation of this parable is found in the verses that immediately follow (verses 49-50):

> So it will be at the end of the age. The angels will come out and separate the evil from the righteous and throw them into the furnace of fire, where there will be weeping and gnashing of teeth.

A very different version of this parable is found in Thomas 8.1-3. Thomas' version tells of a fisherman who finds a very large, fine fish and throws back the little ones. The version in Thomas may be closer to the original, which probably had a message like the parables of the pearl and the hidden treasure. The image of the kingdom being like a fish that has been caught is something that we could expect from Jesus. The fine fish will be eaten, while the little fish will be thrown back and spared. This is the kind of twist that Jesus liked to build into his parables.

The Parable of the Laborers in the Vineyard

This parable is found only in Matthew 20.1-15, and reads as follows:

> For the kingdom of heaven is like a landowner who went out early in the morning to hire laborers for his vineyard. After agreeing with the laborers for the usual daily wage, he sent them into his vineyard. When he went out about nine o'clock, he saw others standing idle in the marketplace; and he said to them, "You also go into the vineyard, and I will pay you whatever is right." So they went. When he went out again about noon and about three o'clock, he did the same. And about five o'clock he went out and found others standing around; and he said to them, "Why are you standing here idle all day?" They said to him, "Because no one has hired us." He said to them, "You also go into the vineyard." When evening came, the owner of the vineyard said to his manager, "Call the laborers and give them their pay, beginning with the last and then going to the first." When those hired about five o'clock came, each of them received the usual daily wage. Now when the first came, they thought they would receive more; but each of them also received the usual daily wage. And when they received it, they grumbled against the land-

owner, saying, "These last worked for only one hour, and you have made them equal to us who have borne the burden of the day and the scorching heat." But he replied to one of them, "Friend, I am doing you no wrong; did you not agree with me for the usual daily wage? Take what belongs to you and go; I choose to give to this last the same as I give to you. Am I not allowed to do what I choose with what belongs to me? Or are you envious because I am generous?"

An important element of Jesus' teaching was an insistence that the law should not become a crutch for your ego; adherence to the law should not be a source of pride because all have sinned. In this parable the workers who were hired early in the day (those who have habitually made an attempt to keep the law) are resentful when the workers hired late in the day (those who have fallen but have recently repented and turned to God) are paid the same wage. The workers who were hired early in the day are essentially exalting themselves at the expense of others, which is the opposite of what God wants.

This parable calls to mind the story of the prodigal son, in which the older brother complains about the generous treatment the prodigal receives upon his return home. Similarly, the workers hired early in the day think they deserve special treatment and are resentful towards the late-comers.

Matthew views this parable as an illustration of the saying, "The last will be first, and the first will be last," and he is correct. Those who exalt themselves at the expense of others will be humbled, and those who humble themselves before God will be exalted because, as Jesus says, "Blessed are the pure in heart, for they will see God" (Matthew 5.8).

This parable would have made sense to Jesus' listeners only if the circumstances it describes were familiar to them, and we might consider the situation in Galilee it implies. The parable's description of a landowner hiring unemployed individuals, or day laborers, who are probably disenfranchised peasants, is consistent with what we know of the economic realities of first century Galilee. There, as elsewhere in the Roman empire, subsistence farming by peasants owning small plots of land was being replaced by large estates geared towards cash crops. This expropriation of resources was seen by Jesus, and the peasants for whom he spoke, as immoral and tyrannical. Unlike his real-life counterparts, however, the landowner in Jesus' ingenious parable pays his workers more than would have expected of him. Jesus' Galilean listeners must have recognized and appreciated this contrast between the ruthless behavior of the landowners they knew and the generous behavior of the parable's landowner.

The Parable of the Wicked Tenants

This parable is found in all the synoptic Gospels (Mark 12.1-9, Matthew 21.33-41 and Luke 20.9-16) and in Thomas 65.1-7. Mark's version is as follows:

> A man planted a vineyard, put a fence around it, dug a pit for the wine press, and built a watchtower; then he leased it to tenants and went to another country. When the season came, he sent a slave to the tenants to collect from them his share of the produce of the vineyard. But they seized him, and beat him, and sent him away empty-handed. And again he sent another slave to them; this one they beat over the head and insulted. Then he sent another, and that one they killed. And so it was with many others; some they beat, and others they killed. He had still one other, a beloved son. Finally he sent him to them, saying, "They will respect my son." But those tenants said to one another, "This is the heir; come let us kill him, and the inheritance will be ours." So they seized him, killed him, and threw him out of the vineyard. What then will the owner of the vineyard do? He will come and destroy the tenants and give the vineyard to others.

This "parable" is an allegory that appears to be based on the Song of the Unfruitful Vineyard in Isaiah 5.1-7. The tenants in charge of the vineyard are the members of the religious establishment in Jerusalem, the vineyard is Israel, the slaves sent by the owner are the prophets, and the son is obviously Jesus. This parable was a popular explanation for why the church had become a Gentile institution and I believe it was created by the early church. I doubt if any of the versions of this parable go back to Jesus, including the version in Thomas, which is the least allegorical of the four.

The Parable of the Ten Bridesmaids

This parable is found only in Matthew 25.1-12, and reads as follows:

> Then the kingdom of heaven will be like this. Ten bridesmaids took their lamps and went to meet the bridegroom. Five of them were foolish, and five were wise. When the foolish took their lamps, they took no oil with them; but the wise took flasks of oil with their lamps. As the bridegroom was delayed, all of them became drowsy and slept. But at midnight there was a shout, "Look! Here is the bridegroom! Come out and meet him." Then all those bridesmaids got up and trimmed their lamps. The foolish said to the wise, "Give us some of your oil, for our lamps are going out." But the wise replied, "No! there will not be enough for you and for us; you had better go to the dealers and buy some for yourselves." And while they went to buy it, the bridegroom came, and those who were ready went with him into the wedding banquet; and the door was shut. Later the other bridesmaids came also, saying, "Lord, lord, open to us." But he replied, "Truly I tell you, I do not know you."

This is one of those parables in which an interpretation is provided. The moral of the story is: Keep awake because you don't know when Jesus may return. This is the theme of a number of sayings in the latter part of Matthew that deal with being prepared for the second coming.

It is hard to see this story as a parable of Jesus. It is predictable, the selfish behavior of the wise bridesmaids isn't particularly inspirational, the details are a little ridiculous (Was there a 24-hour lamp oil store in the neighborhood?), and it fits with Matthew's agenda a little too neatly. The five foolish bridesmaids probably went to the same place that Matthew sent the poor guy who showed up at the great feast without his wedding robe—"the outer darkness, where there will be weeping and gnashing of teeth" (Matthew 22.13).

The Parable of the Banquet Seats

This parable is found only at Luke 14.8-10, and reads as follows:

> When you are invited by someone to a wedding banquet, do not sit down at the place of honor, in case someone more distinguished than you has been invited by your host; and the host who invited both of you may come and say to you, "Give this person your place," and then in disgrace you would start to take the lowest place. But when you are invited, go and sit down at the lowest place, so that when your host comes, he may say to you, "Friend, move up higher"; then you will be honored in the presence of all who sit at the table with you.

This parable is similar to Proverbs 25.6-7, which reads, "Do not put yourself forward in the king's presence or stand in the place of the great; for it is better to be told, 'Come up here,' than to be put lower in the presence of a noble."

This parable is not just a lesson in social etiquette. Luke often portrays the kingdom as a feast, and to enter the kingdom of God, to come into God's presence, you must humble yourself: "Those who humble themselves will be exalted."

The message of this parable is essentially identical to that of Matthew 20.1-15, the parable about the workers who are hired throughout the day. The message is simple: You should not be seduced by a sense of pride in your own accomplishments.

The Parable of the Dishonest Manager

This parable, which is found only in Luke 16.1-8, has traditionally been viewed as one of the most difficult of all Jesus' parables. It has always been a source of embarrassment for Christians because it seems to encourage devious, self-serving behavior. The parable reads as follows:

> Then Jesus said to his disciples, "There was a rich man who had a manager, and charges were brought to him that this man was squandering his property. So he summoned him and said to him, 'What is this that I hear about you? Give me an accounting of your management, because you cannot be my manager any longer.' Then the manager said to himself, 'What will I do, now that my master is taking the position away from me? I am not strong enough to dig, and I am ashamed to beg. I have decided what to do so that, when I am dismissed as manager, people may welcome me into their homes.' So, summoning his master's debtors one by one, he asked the first, 'How much do you owe my master?' He answered, 'A hundred jugs of olive oil.' He said to him, 'Take your bill, sit down quickly, and make it fifty.' Then he asked another, 'And how much do you owe?' He replied, 'A hundred containers of wheat.' He said to him, 'Take your bill and make it eighty.' And his master commended the dishonest manager because he had acted shrewdly; for the children of this age are more shrewd in dealing with their own generation than are the children of light."

It is obvious that Luke doesn't know what this parable

means. He gives three different interpretations right after the parable, and concludes his muddled analysis with the words, "You cannot serve God and wealth," which is a favorite theme of his.[4]

In this parable, the manager, or steward, is an individual responsible for administering the master's estate. The master, who is a good man, has received word from someone in the community that his manager has been dishonest. Consequently, the master decides to dismiss the manager. He confronts him with the accusation, demands an accounting of the manager's activity, and tells him he is to be dismissed.

Two things are notable about the charges and the manager's response to them. First, the master could have the manager thrown into prison for defrauding him. Instead, he simply intends to fire the manager. He is being generous. Second, when confronted with the accusations of impropriety, the manager doesn't deny the charges; he acknowledges them by his silence.

The manager may have been dishonest in his dealings with his master, but he certainly is honest with himself. He recognizes that he is in serious trouble and faced with some unattractive options, so he quickly decides on a plan of action. He calls the master's debtors and proceeds to give them what amounts to huge discounts on the amounts they owe the master. These debtors are, most likely, tenants on the master's estate who owe him some portion of their produce, and the manager is reducing the "take" that the master is to receive.

It is easy to get the impression that, in granting these discounts, the manager is doing something that he is unauthorized to do. However, if the tenants had any suspicions that the manager's actions were not approved by the master they would not go along. To do this would jeopardize their position with the master and the tenants would have no interest in doing that. Thus, they are not colluding with the manager to further cheat the master. They believe they are simply recipients of the master's goodwill and he has authorized the discounts.

The manager has moved quickly, and by the time the master realizes what has happened, he is being praised throughout the community as a generous man for granting the huge discounts. Under these circumstances, if he fires the manager and acknowledges that he did not authorize the discounts he will lose face with the community. Instead, he decides to praise the manager for acting so shrewdly and let the manager's actions go unpunished.

In this story, the manager has been put in a desperate position by his unacceptable behavior and then saves himself by relying on the generous nature of his master. His plan would work only if the master were a good man who would not punish him, and his faith in his master is justified at the end of the story.

The message of this parable is that, when faced with impending judgment, it is best to rely on God's mercy and his willingness to forgive. The parable shows Jesus' brilliance in storytelling; he has converted what could be a sanctimonious threat of judgment and demand for obedience into what must have been a delightful story for many of his poorer listeners.

The Parable of the Prodigal Son

This parable is found only in Luke 15.11-32, and reads as follows:

> Then Jesus said, "There was a man who had two sons. The younger of them said to his father, 'Father, give me the share of the property that will belong to me.' So he divided his property between them. A few days later the younger son gathered all he had and traveled to a distant country, and there he squandered his property in dissolute living. When he had spent everything, a severe famine took place through-

out that country, and he began to be in need. So he went and hired himself out to one of the citizens of that country, who sent him to his fields to feed the pigs. He would gladly have filled himself with the pods the pigs were eating; and no one gave him anything. But when he came to himself he said, 'How many of my father's hired hands have bread enough and to spare, but here I am dying of hunger! I will get up and go to my father, and I will say to him, "Father, I have sinned against heaven and before you; I am no longer worthy to be called your son; treat me like one of your hired hands."' So he set off and went to his father. But while he was still far off, his father saw him and was filled with compassion; he ran and put his arms around him and kissed him. Then the son said to him, 'Father, I have sinned against heaven and before you; I am no longer worthy to be called your son.' But the father said to his slaves, 'Quickly, bring out a robe—the best one—and put it on him; put a ring on his finger and sandals on his feet. And get the fatted calf and kill it, and let us eat and celebrate; for this son of mine was dead and is alive again; he was lost and is found!' And they began to celebrate.

"Now his elder son was in the field; and when he came and approached the house, he heard music and dancing. He called one of the slaves and asked what was going on. He replied, 'Your brother has come, and your father has killed the fatted calf, because he has got him back safe and sound.' Then he became angry and refused to go in. His father came out and began to plead with him. But he answered his father, 'Listen! For all these years I have been working like a slave for you, and I have never disobeyed your command; yet you have never given me even a young goat so that I might celebrate with my friends. But when this son of yours came back, who has devoured your property with prostitutes, you killed the fatted calf for him!' Then the father said to him, 'Son, you are always with me, and all that is mine is yours. But we had to celebrate and rejoice, because this brother of yours was dead and has come back to life; he was lost and has been found.'"

The prodigal son is one of Jesus' most famous stories and it is easy to see why. It is a compelling story of estrangement, forgiveness, and reconciliation.

It is useful to consider the story's social context.[5] The episode the story describes would probably have taken place in a small village in rural Galilee, and the village's community would be closer than in the large cities so common in modern society. This has an important bearing on the story and the father's actions, as the following analysis should show.

The story begins with the younger of two sons requesting his inheritance from his father. In middle eastern societies, the son's request would be seen as an insult to the father; it is as if the son had said, "I can't wait for you to die." The father responds to his son's request by dividing his property between both of his sons, as is clear from the statement that "he divided his property between *them*." The granting of the son's impertinent request by the father is an extraordinary action, and would not be customary. The expected reaction to such a request would be outrage and rejection.

The absence of any action by the older brother as the request is made and granted is significant. The older brother doesn't sell his property as the younger one does, but he seems to accept the transfer without objection. Also, the older son would be expected to make an attempt at reconciling his father and brother, but no such effort appears to have been made. The lack of action here is consistent with the later reaction of the older son to his brother's treatment upon his return.

Next, the younger son sells his property. We are told that he did this hastily—within a "few days." It isn't likely that anyone in the village would buy it from him since this would be an insult to the father. Consequently, the son probably sold the land to an outsider. In modern societies it is easy to miss the significance of what the younger son has done. He has not only insulted his father with his outrageous request, but has disgraced himself in the eyes of the community by hastily selling his land. This irresponsible action would be seen as a rejection of his ties to the community as well as his relations with his father and brother.

The son goes to a foreign land and squanders his money. After his money is gone a famine strikes and he is reduced to working as the servant of a Gentile, feeding pigs and eating their food. This is about as bad as it gets for a Jew in Jesus' time. In this desperate situation the son decides to return home and ask his father to take him on as a "hired hand."

It is easy to get the impression that this plan to ask for treatment as a hired hand is an expression of humility, but maybe the son just figures he can't pay back the money he squandered so he will settle for being a servant. However, when he gets home he finds out that his father doesn't care about the money, but just wants his son back.

The son would have expected that, when he returned to his village, he would be ridiculed and ostracized. However, this beats starving so he heads for home. As he approaches the village his father sees him. The father immediately runs to his son and kisses him. This behavior would have been more than a little undignified, but the father's only concern is his son. The father rushes to his son and publicly embraces him, thus sparing him the ordeal of being ridiculed by the community.

The father orders his servants to put the best robe on his son. The "best robe" is most likely the father's, the one that he would wear at an important social gathering. He tells the servants to put a ring on his son's finger and shoes on his feet. By giving these instructions to his servants the father has reestablished his son's place in his home. In light of this response by the father, how could the son then ask to be a hired hand in his father's home?

The father tells his servants to kill the fatted calf so that he can celebrate his son's return. The fact that a calf will be slaughtered indicates the celebration will include the entire community. Otherwise, the father would have ordered that a smaller animal, such as a goat or lamb, be killed. By publicly embracing his son, attiring him in his finest robe, and holding a feast for the entire community to celebrate his son's return, the father has attempted to reconcile his son with the community.

The older son doesn't respond to all this like a member of the family; he responds like a resentful hired hand. He calls his brother, "that son of yours," and refuses to come in to the banquet. This behavior would have been very inappropriate in middle eastern culture since the older brother would be expected, at a minimum, to come in, help with the guests, and make his complaints known in private after the banquet ended. Instead, the older brother insults his father by making him come outside to plead with him.

The father's response to the older son is just like his response to the prodigal. He doesn't explode with anger, but just tells him that he loves him and that there could be only one reaction to his brother's return. This one reaction is total, unconditional acceptance and love, and this is the central theme of this parable.

We should note that the issue of the law clearly is raised in this parable. The older son feels like he is entitled to something special because, as he tells his father, "I have never disobeyed your command." This is the kind of entitlement mentality that Jesus railed against. The prodigal son tells the same story found in the parable of the Pharisee and the tax collector using different circumstances. The younger son has sinned and he knows he is unworthy; the older son feels he has vindicated himself by doing what he is told. For Jesus, God's forgiveness is freely available; it cannot be earned.

A question regarding "atonement" often seems to come up when this parable is discussed. It is possible to take the position that, by leaving his house and humbly dealing with his sons, the father's actions represents the ministry of Jesus. I don't have a problem with this and I think Jesus' ministry shows up in a lot of his parables. However, I don't think we should stretch things by saying this parable, or any of the other parables of Jesus, says anything about an "atoning death on the cross" that makes salvation possible. To make such an assertion is to read things into Jesus' parables that simply aren't there. Even the most blatantly allegorical and "Christianized" parable—the parable of the wicked tenants—doesn't say anything about the son's death being one that makes atonement possible. This is simply a non-issue in Jesus' parables.

I've often wondered if any of Jesus' parables are, in some sense, autobiographical. I don't believe the parable of the prodigal son is autobiographical in any literal sense, but in a spiritual sense it may be. Christians believe Jesus was sinless and this is what makes his atoning death on the cross possible. This idea is based on the requirements in Leviticus for sacrificial animals to be "without blemish." Christians also believe that Jesus could identify with the needs of sinners because he was God in the flesh. However, it seems more likely that Jesus talked about saving lost sheep because this was his own story. This isn't the message that anyone wants to get from Jesus' parables but it makes more sense than trying to find an atoning sacrificial death in them.

Jesus tells many parables that have a message similar to that of the prodigal son. The parables of the laborers in the vineyard, the woman who lost a silver coin (Luke 15.8-9), the lost sheep (Matthew 18.12-14 and Luke 15.3-6) and the two sons (Matthew 21.28-30) are examples. Clearly, the message of God's unconditional love, which was available even to sinners, was an important feature of Jesus' message. It was the "good news" that Jesus proclaimed. For Jesus, God's love was there, and it was irresistible. There was nothing you could do to earn it. The only appropriate response to the grace of God was humble acceptance and submission.

Only One Thing Is Important

When Jesus visits Martha and Mary (Luke 10.38-42), Martha scolds Mary for ignoring her chores and listening to Jesus instead. Jesus tells her, "Martha, Martha, you are worried and distracted by many things; there is need of only one thing." For Jesus, the only thing that mattered was the kingdom of God. All of the things that motivate and sustain so many people—material possessions, family ties, social status—these had lost their relevance for Jesus. He rejected the superficiality of the religious life of his people in uncompromising terms, and called upon them to "love the Lord your God with all your heart, and with all your soul, and with all your strength, and with all your mind; and your neighbor as yourself" (Luke 10.27). For Jesus, this was all that mattered.

Jesus' total devotion to God and his fellow man permeates his teaching. This devotion, this singlemindedness of purpose, led Jesus to view the daily affairs that involve so many of us as meaningless trivialities. He tells his followers (Matthew 5.39-42):

> ...if anyone strikes you on the right cheek, turn the other also; and if anyone wants to sue you and take your coat, give your cloak as well; and if anyone forces you to go one mile, go also the second mile. Give to everyone who begs from you, and do not refuse anyone who wants to borrow from you.

For Jesus, the petty disputes that give rise to these types of conflicts simply don't matter. The only thing that matters is to "give to everyone."

Jesus tells his followers not to strive for the things that "the heathen" run after, such as clothing and food. In the Lord's Prayer, he says we should ask, first, for God's kingdom, and then only for "our daily bread." He doesn't look for the things that attract so many people, but sees them as distractions. When he is free from these distractions he notices things other people skip over. He says of the "lilies of the field," that "even Solomon in all his glory was not clothed like one of these" (Matthew 6.28-29). Jesus' devotion to the kingdom has totally set him free; he is free to forgive, to love, and to find the presence of God in things that are taken for granted by everyone else.

Jesus' teaching was profound, radical, and uncompromising. As a result, when it comes to its practical application it has been almost universally watered-down or ignored. How many people actually turn the other cheek, "lend" with no expectation of being repaid, see no value in material possessions, and have devotion to God that takes precedence over career, social status and family relationships? Not many.

In connection with Jesus' teaching and his hopes for what might happen after his death, it is interesting to consider two related parables (Luke 5.36-39):

> He also told them a parable: "No one tears a piece from a new garment and sews it on an old garment; otherwise the new will be torn, and the piece from the new will not match the old. And no one puts new wine into old wineskins; otherwise the new wine will burst the skins and be spilled, and the skins will be destroyed. But new wine must be put into fresh wineskins. And no one after drinking old wine desires new wine, but says, 'The old is good.'"

Traditionally, these two parables have been interpreted to mean that Jesus' new, vital religion (Christianity) must be separated from the old, outdated, ossified religion of Judaism, but we might consider a less provincial interpretation.

Garments were torn in Jesus' time as a sign of mourning. In the parable about the inappropriate patching of a rent garment, Jesus is telling his disciples to mourn him after his death, and to honor his memory. How were they to honor his memory? Jesus tells them not to become drunk on innovation, but to respect the traditions on which his teaching was based. Jesus isn't saying the religion of his ancestors is now invalid. After all, he knows that, "The old wine is good." Jesus wants his disciples to understand and teach his own unique interpretation of the law but to remain faithful to the traditional religion of Israel.

Was this advice heeded? In many respects, Jesus' followers were faithful to his teaching. For example, a close connection between love of God and love of man is central to Christian belief, just as it was central to Jesus' own message. In one important respect, however, Jesus' followers seem to have changed his message: They replaced repentance, and reliance on the mercy of God, with faith in Jesus as savior. This isn't surprising given the uncompromising nature of Jesus' message, the rejection of Jesus' ministry by Israel, and the transformation of the church into a Gentile institution.

It is easy for us, almost 2,000 years later, to suggest that Jesus' followers in the first century should have done things differently, or to accuse them of being unfaithful to his original message. However, these people endured great hardships and the fact that Christianity survived as a religion was due only to their devotion to Jesus. This devotion isn't something for which I'm inclined to criticize them.

5

JESUS' MINISTRY

Jesus and John the Baptist

John the Baptist played an influential role in Jesus' life, and all the Gospels place the two men together at the beginning of Jesus' ministry. John the Baptist was a charismatic figure who, like Jesus, was both enormously popular with the people and a threat to the religious establishment. In Luke 7.29, Jesus is talking to a crowd of people and we are told that, "all the people...had been baptized with John's baptism," except the Pharisees and lawyers, who refused. John was a threat to the religious establishment for the same reason he was popular with the people—he didn't rely on booklearning or the technicalities of the law for his authority, but spoke from his heart.

The Gospels' portrayal of John indicates their accounts are designed to exalt Jesus and minimize the importance of the Baptist. Even the one statement of Jesus in which he praises John by saying (Matthew 11.11), "Truly I tell you, among those born of women no one has arisen greater than John the Baptist," has the following disclaimer attached to it: "yet the least in the kingdom of heaven is greater than he." Based on the way John gets treated in the Gospels it is entirely possible that the first part is something that Jesus actually said, while the second is something that was appended later by Jesus' followers.

The stories told about Jesus in the Gospels may not always be historical but they often tell us something important about his life. Jesus' experience at his baptism is an example of this. The synoptic Gospels all tell us that, at or around the time of his baptism, Jesus had some type of powerful religious experience in which he saw the heavens open and heard God's voice. This is the early church's version of Jesus' "call" to begin his ministry.

The baptism of Jesus by John was clearly an embarrassment for the early church, because John baptized as a sign of repentance and those who came typically "confessed their sins" during the process (Matthew 3.6). Consequently, we see a development in the Gospel tradition that seeks to minimize the importance of the event or ignore it completely. In Mark, the baptism is simply mentioned, while Matthew has John try to talk Jesus out of it by saying, "I need to be baptized by you, and do you come to me?" (Matt. 3.14) In Luke, Jesus is baptized, but apparently only after John is put in prison. John's Gospel doesn't even mention the baptism. Instead, at its beginning John calls Jesus, "the Lamb of God who takes away the sin of the world! This is he of whom I said, 'After me comes a man who ranks ahead of me because he was before me'" (John 1.29-30).

It is likely that the relationship between Jesus and John the Baptist has been minimized in other important respects.

Jesus is recorded in Mark and Matthew as being in the wilderness until John's arrest. This implies that Jesus' stay in the desert may have been related to John's activity somehow.

In the synoptic Gospels Jesus is said to have spent forty days in the wilderness after his baptism. Luke says that Jesus ate nothing during this period and both Matthew and Luke record hunger as one of Jesus' temptations. This account might actually refer to a period during which Jesus, like John, practiced an ascetic lifestyle in the wilderness. Jesus could even have been an active disciple of John at some point.

As Jesus began his ministry, John's Gospel says that Jesus took some of John's disciples with him (one of whom was Andrew, Peter's brother), and that Jesus' disciples baptized during the early part of his ministry. In addition, Mark says that John's message was essentially identical to the message that Jesus first preached. In light of these factors it seems that John significantly influenced Jesus as he began his ministry.

It has been suggested that Jesus' ministry was a parting of the ways for the two men. After all, Jesus rejected fasting and the ascetic lifestyle espoused by John. Jesus also went into the villages, seeking the lost sheep of the house of Israel, while John appears to have remained in the wilderness and let the people come to him. On the other hand, it is possible that Jesus and John saw their ministries as complementary in some way.

The Gospels tell us that John was imprisoned by Herod because he had chastised him for his relations with Herodias (the wife of Philip, Herod's brother). He was then executed by Herod to fulfill an oath made after a particularly "pleasing" dance by Herodias' daughter, Salome (Mark 6.21-28). However, Josephus, the Jewish historian, tells us that John was executed because of his influence with the people and that Herod was afraid his ministry would lead to a disturbance or larger revolt. It may be that both factors played a role in John's death.

One has to wonder what effect John's execution must

have had on Jesus. The men seem to have been close until John's death, as implied by the statement in Matthew 14.12 that, after John's disciples buried him, they came and told Jesus what had happened. Jesus must have seen the writing on the wall long before he went to Jerusalem for his final Passover, and John's death probably led to him to question the purpose and direction of his ministry.

We might ask why, if Jesus didn't baptize, baptism seemed to be a feature of the church's ritual life from its beginning (Acts 2.38) and why baptism was so important to the church's concept of the holy spirit's activity (see Acts 1.5). Although the synoptic Gospels are silent about the issue, it is possible that Jesus actually did baptize throughout his ministry but this has been left out to separate him from John. Maybe it isn't a coincidence that Jesus always seems to be near water in Mark's Gospel.

We might also consider the possibility that Jesus' disciples were a lot closer to John than the Gospels would have us know. In Acts 1.21-22, as Peter is giving the requirements necessary for the replacement of Judas, he says this man must be, "one of the men who have accompanied us during all the time that the Lord Jesus went in and out among us, beginning from the baptism of John until the day when he was taken up from us." This statement makes it sound like a lot of the disciples were with Jesus when he was with John. This isn't quite the way the Gospels tell the story, but it is still a possibility.

Jesus and his Disciples

The traditional view is that Jesus called twelve men to be his disciples, these disciples deserted him when he was arrested in Jerusalem, and he appeared to these same disciples (eleven of them anyway) after his resurrection. This traditional view sees the disciples in sort of a static, unified way—twelve were called, they fell away, Jesus appeared to them later. This picture is a little oversimplified.

The Gospels indicate that more than twelve disciples followed Jesus. Mark 2.15 tells us that, "as he sat at dinner in Levi's house, many tax collectors and sinners were also sitting with Jesus and his disciples—for there were many who followed him." This suggests that more than twelve disciples followed Jesus. Luke 6.13 is more explicit. It tells us that Jesus picked the twelve from a larger number of disciples: "And when day came, he called his disciples and chose twelve of them, whom he also named apostles." Also, in Luke 10.1-12 Jesus sends out a group of seventy, or seventy-two, disciples, depending on the manuscript used, so Luke clearly says that Jesus had more than twelve disciples.

It is possible that Jesus had many disciples but an inner circle of twelve. However, Mark 4.10-11 says, "When he was alone, those who were around him along with the twelve asked him about the parables. And he said to them, 'To you has been given the secret of the kingdom of God.'" The implication of this statement is that Jesus' inner circle of disciples included more than just "the twelve."

Jesus' ministry seems to have consisted of two distinct phases. In the first phase Jesus roamed Galilee teaching to large crowds and healing. Then, once he decided to go to Jerusalem and give himself up to be killed, Jesus stopped his healing activity and started working more with his disciples so he could prepare them for his death. There appears to have been a change in the way his message was received at this point; many who had previously followed him began to fall away. Once his disciples realized what he planned to do, many became disillusioned and left. This is implied in John 6.66, which says, "because of this [Jesus' teaching about being the bread of life] many of his disciples turned back and no longer went about with him."

By the time Jesus got to Jerusalem it is possible that many of his disciples had already deserted him. When he was arrested even his closest disciples ran for their lives. Thus, the disciples may not have been a stable unit of twelve from call to desertion, but a larger, more diverse group that dwindled to a dedicated inner circle as Jesus' ministry drew to a close. It may be that the designation of the disciples as "the twelve" was given, not at the beginning of Jesus' ministry, but to the faithful remnant who remained with him to the end. As the end of his career approached, Jesus may have begun referring to his disciples as the twelve because he saw them, in some sense, as the "true Israel."

It should be noted that Jesus attracted a large number of women followers, although none of the Gospel writers seems particularly interested in calling them disciples. In Luke 8.2-3 Jesus is accompanied by "some women who had been cured of evil spirits and infirmities: Mary, called Magdalene, from whom seven demons had gone out, and Joanna, the wife of Herod's steward Chuza, and Susanna, and many others, who provided for them out of their resources." At least some of these women appear to have remained devoted followers of Jesus to the end.

Healings, Exorcisms and Miracles

When confronted with the healing activity and exorcisms of Jesus, many people believe there are two possibilities. First, we can believe that these things happened as they are written and are signs confirming the church's understanding of Jesus as the Son of God, God incarnate, etc. Alternatively, we can reject this aspect of Jesus' ministry as a fabrication, a falsehood based on a primitive understanding of the world that has been invalidated by modern science.

I believe this is a false choice. The world is not so tidy that it can be divided into black and white like this, particularly when we get into the realm of human experience that pushes the borders of our understanding. The actual range of possibilities is much wider and more mysterious than we imagine.

Still, each of us has to draw the line of believability somewhere. Drawing it in the middle ground is a little arbitrary, but that is what I intend to do. I believe some type of healing activity took place, but it isn't useful to go into the details and try to figure out exactly what diseases or deformities Jesus might have been curing. I don't believe Jesus' healings were done from a distance, accomplished simply by the utterance of a single word or command, or that Jesus brought dead people back to life.

I don't believe in demonic possession either, and don't place a whole lot of importance on this type of activity. It was important to Jesus, though, who saw his exorcisms as an assault on the power of Satan. He summed up his view of this activity with the following comment: "no one can enter a strong man's house and plunder his property without first tying up the strong man; then indeed the house can be plundered" (Mark 3.27). The strong man here is Satan, and Jesus, in his ministry, is tying him up and plundering his property. Exorcisms almost certainly took place, but I don't feel inclined to speculate on what was really happening during these events.

The Gospels make it seem that healings and exorcisms were easy for Jesus. He simply says something like, "OK, you're healed." However, in a couple of instances some degree of difficulty is indicated. First, in Mark 8.22-26 Jesus restores a blind man's sight. He rubs his spit around the man's eyes, but when Jesus says, "Can you see anything?" the man says, "I can see people, but they look like trees, walking." Jesus has to lay his hands on the man's eyes again before his vision is completely restored. In the exorcism recorded at Mark 9.14-29, Jesus' disciples are unable to cast out a demon. Jesus has to intervene and suggests to his disciples that this demon was tougher than others. He tells them (Mark 9.29), "This kind can come out only through prayer." It appears from these episodes that healings and exorcisms weren't always easy.

It is possible that, when Jesus healed or performed exorcisms, he entered some type of ecstatic state or trance; it may not have been simply a matter of casually saying a couple of words, but a powerful experience that gripped both the healer and the healed. It would have been quite a sight and it is no surprise that Jesus' healing activity drew large crowds.

Two episodes support the assertion that Jesus entered some kind of ecstatic state while healing. First, in Mark 3.21 we learn that, "When his family heard it [that he was going into trances while healing, possibly], they went out to restrain him, for people were saying, 'He has gone out of his mind.'" Then, in the following verses, some scribes accuse Jesus of casting out Satan with Satan. The concern that Jesus was losing his mind or working with Satan is the type of reaction one might expect if Jesus was entering an ecstatic state as he healed or performed exorcisms. It is no wonder that people who witnessed this activity would say something like what we find in Luke 5.26: "we have seen strange things today."

When you read the Gospels and consider the effect that Jesus' healings and exorcisms must have had on people, it is easy to see how this aspect of Jesus' ministry could lead to a circus atmosphere. I believe that Jesus became disillusioned with the response of people to this activity and decided it was counterproductive.

A couple of statements support this view. First, Jesus says (Luke 16.16): "The law and the prophets were in effect until John came; since then the good news of the kingdom of God is proclaimed, and everyone tries to enter it by force." Many have wondered what this statement means. If you think about the way things probably transpired when the crowds gathered around Jesus as he healed, there likely was often a free-for-all as people jostled for position to get close to him, and that the stronger tended to push aside the weaker. If this is the case, it is easy to see how Jesus might feel these people were taking advantage of him and disregarding the needs of others. I believe that, when the dust settled on Jesus' healing ministry, he expressed his disillusionment with the following words: (Matthew 7.6) "Do not give what is holy to dogs; and do not throw your pearls before swine, or they will trample them under foot and turn and maul you."

The Gospels all have us believe that faith played an important part in Jesus' healing activity, and that the faith of the healed individual made the healing possible. However, there is one notable instance where healing definitely isn't based on the faith of the person healed. This healing is performed, not by Jesus, but by Peter. In this case, a crippled beggar was "expecting to receive something" from Peter and John (Acts 3.5). The man was looking for a handout and was healed instead! In all probability nothing was required of those who were healed except a request for it to happen.

I've already indicated that I believe the miracles told about Jesus (walking on water, etc.) are legendary in nature and not historical events. However, these stories can tell us some interesting things about how Jesus was understood by his followers. For example, consider the imagery used in the feeding of the multitudes. There were twelve tribes of Israel, and there were twelve baskets of leftovers after the 5,000 were fed. Mark 8.2 tells us the 4,000 had been with Jesus for three days. This is the number of days' journey by which the ark of the covenant preceded Israel as it left Sinai (Numbers 10.33). The hungry multitudes were fed miraculously in the wilderness, which recalls the hunger of the Israelites during their journey to the promised land and the manna from heaven that was provided for them. In Luke 9.14, Jesus has the disciples make the people sit down in groups of about fifty, while Mark 6.40 has groups of hundreds and fifties. Similarly, in Numbers, Moses groups the people into thousands, hundreds, fifties and tens (Exodus 18.25), and assigns officers to hear their complaints. Thus, this story portrays Jesus as a new Moses, providing for his people in the wilderness. These symbols and parallels show how the life of Jesus was understood, and the miracles possibly constructed, using the raw materials provided in scripture.

"The Son of Man has nowhere to lay his head"

Many people have this image of a gentle Jesus giving a sermon to a rapt audience, or a commanding Jesus ordering out demons and healing people with a word or a touch of his hand. Then, when Jesus gets to Jerusalem, his enemies come to get him under cover of darkness, as he is betrayed by one of his disciples. However, there are many indications in the Gospels that things weren't all sweetness and light up until the time Jesus was crucified.

Jesus was a polarizing figure. He was, by all accounts, a young man who railed at the hypocrisy and greed of his elders. He was an unlettered, charismatic Galilean who spoke on his own authority, and challenged the defenders of the status quo who derived what authority they had from books and tradition. He openly associated with the most ostracized and powerless members of society. He preached that the exalted would be humbled and the humble exalted. He demanded total commitment to his message of the kingdom and left no room for compromise or second thoughts. Consequently, Jesus made lots of enemies.

In Matthew 8.19-20 a scribe says to Jesus, "Teacher, I will follow you wherever you go." Jesus replied, "Foxes have holes, and birds of the air have nests; but the Son of Man has nowhere to lay his head." Many people skip over these verses without really thinking about them. They figure Jesus is simply referring to the fact that he wanders from town to town proclaiming his message. However, there may be more to this statement. Jesus might be saying that he is on the run, so to speak. Given the charismatic and uncompromising nature of his message, Jesus' ministry appears to have been a dangerous enterprise.

After Jesus began his ministry, John the Baptist was killed by Herod Antipas for preaching the kingdom of God, and throughout the Gospels we find people, such as Pharisees, Herodians and others, who want to kill Jesus. In Luke 9.7-9, we find that even Herod is "perplexed" about Jesus and "tried to see him." It isn't likely that Herod wanted to hear a sermon; he probably wanted to kill Jesus just as he killed John.

In addition, it seems Jesus' enemies weren't the only people who caused problems for him; the crowds that surrounded him wherever he went could apparently get pretty rough sometimes. Jesus is constantly going off somewhere by himself, or at least trying to. At Luke 5.15-16 we find that, "more than ever the word about Jesus spread abroad; many crowds would gather to hear him and to be cured of their diseases. But he would withdraw to deserted places and pray." After feeding the 5,000, according to John 6.15, "When Jesus realized that they were about to come and take him by force to make him king, he withdrew again to the mountain by himself."

It seems that everyone wanted something from Jesus: They wanted him to heal them, they wanted to make him king, or they wanted him dead.

Why did Jesus seem to avoid the larger towns in Galilee? Why was he always on the move? Why is he constantly trying to get away from crowds? Why does he seem to be so secretive in the synoptic Gospels about who he is and what he is trying to do? It is easy to get the impression that Jesus was at least a little harried and found it safer to be a moving target. It is no wonder that, at one point, Jesus would groan something like, "you faithless generation, how much longer must I be among you? How much longer must I put up with you?" (Mark 9.19)

I don't mean to create the impression that Jesus was pushed around a lot and always stressed out. His ministry was clearly tumultuous and controversial, but this doesn't mean Jesus was helplessly swept along with the current. I believe this is the message that is sent by stories like the calming of the storm. In Mark 4.35-40, Jesus "rebukes" a storm, to the amazement of his disciples. I don't think that Jesus really calmed a storm, but this story may tell us how his disciples thought he handled the events surrounding his ministry. The story implies that Jesus chose his own destiny, and that he was not at the mercy of forces he couldn't control.

The Transfiguration

The transfiguration is one of those stories in which powerful images are used to recall an important event in the life of Jesus and his disciples. I believe the story of the transfiguration provides some significant insights into the way Jesus and his disciples understood his ministry. The transfiguration is described in Mark 9.2-8 as follows:

> Six days later, Jesus took with him Peter and James and John, and led them up a high mountain apart, by themselves. And he was transfigured before them, and his clothes became dazzling white, such as no one on earth could bleach them. And there appeared to them Elijah with Moses, who were talking with Jesus. Then Peter said to Jesus, "Rabbi, it is good for us to be here; let us make three dwellings, one for you, one for Moses, and one for Elijah." He did not know what to say, for they were terrified. Then a cloud overshadowed them, and from the cloud there came a voice, "This is my Son, the Beloved; listen to him!" Suddenly when they looked around, they saw no one with them any more, but only Jesus.

The episode is also recorded at Matthew 17.1-8 and Luke 9.28-36.

The transfiguration is recorded primarily as an experience of the disciples. However, I believe this account is the early church's recollection of something that happened to Jesus—something that had a significant impact on the direction of his ministry and was later remembered and described by the disciples in the light of their Easter experience.

I don't accept the storybook version of Jesus' ministry that says he knew from day one exactly what he was going to do, when he was going to do it, and what would follow as a consequence of his actions. I believe that, like any other human being Jesus asked questions, sought answers, and even changed his mind from time to time. I believe the transfiguration recalls the pivotal moment when Jesus decided to go to Jerusalem and give up his life. The account shows that this wasn't some type of casual decision, but was a profound religious experience for Jesus that was shared only with his closest disciples.

I have many reasons for the above conclusions. First, regarding the nature of this experience, the Gospel accounts state that the transfiguration occurred while Jesus was praying with his disciples on a mountaintop and that they entered abruptly into the presence of God (signified by the cloud and heavenly voice). When God speaks, his words are essentially identical to those spoken at Jesus' baptism; they indicate that Jesus once again heard God's call.

This revelation is reinforced by the appearance of Moses and Elijah, which indicates that Jesus was led to this experience, and his subsequent actions, by his reading of the law and the prophets. This is consistent with the fact that, in Matthew and Mark, immediately after the transfiguration Jesus and his disciples begin a conversation about Elijah in which Jesus asks (Mark 9.12), "How then is it written about the Son of Man, that he is to go through many sufferings and be treated with contempt?"

The transfiguration occurs in the Gospel accounts before Jesus began to go to Jerusalem to meet his death. This indicates that, prior to this event, Jesus had not decided on this course of action. It is no coincidence that the account of the transfiguration is closely connected with the beginning of Jesus' set of three predictions about his suffering, death and resurrection. In addition, Luke says that Jesus, Moses and Elijah were, "speaking of his departure, which he was about to accomplish at Jerusalem" (Luke 9.31).

The accounts contain a reference to dwellings, tents, booths, or tabernacles that Peter wants to build for Jesus, Moses and Elijah. Also, Luke has the event take place eight days after Jesus first stated he would be killed. These are references to the Jewish Festival of Booths, which is an eight day harvest celebration in the fall. It is possible that this revelation came to Jesus during or around the time of the Festival of Booths. In this connection, in John 7.8-9 Jesus tells his disciples to go to the Festival of Booths without him since it isn't yet his time. However, Jesus subsequently changes his mind and goes to the festival, albeit secretly. Maybe it was at this time that his destiny was revealed to him.

It is possible that the agonies in Gethsemane recall a night during which Jesus struggled over his destiny and which culminated in the transfiguration experience. The chronology of the Gospels isn't reliable and Jesus' prayer in Gethsemane might not have happened just before his arrest. It may be no coincidence that, according to Matthew and Mark, in Gethsemane Jesus is accompanied by the same disciples—Peter, James and John—that were present at the transfiguration or that, according to Luke, the disciples are struggling to stay awake at both of these momentous events; the transfiguration probably took place after a long, agonizing night of fervent prayer.

It is significant that John's Gospel contains no account of the transfiguration. This is consistent with the fact that, in this Gospel, Jesus never has any doubts about who he is or what he is doing, but is always in complete control of everything. Also, Jesus doesn't agonize over his fate in Gethsemane, but prays that *his disciples* will have the strength to endure the coming ordeal. It is no wonder the transfiguration is missing from the fourth Gospel—there was no need for it.

6

THE PASSION

The Triumphal Entry
and the Cleansing of the Temple

Jesus is said to have entered Jerusalem for his final Passover riding a donkey. This method of entry is portrayed in Matthew as the fulfillment of a prophecy at Zechariah 9.9, which says:

> Rejoice greatly, O daughter Zion!
> Shout aloud, O daughter Jerusalem!
> Lo, your king comes to you;
> triumphant and victorious is he,

humble and riding on a donkey,
on a colt, the foal of a donkey.

As Jesus enters the city, the people who accompany him shout out a passage from Psalms 118.25-26 (per Mark 11.9-10):

Hosanna!
Blessed is the one who comes in
the name of the Lord!
Blessed is the coming kingdom
of our ancestor David!
Hosanna in the highest heaven!

It has been suggested that, because the prophecy in Zechariah is a rather isolated one, and doesn't fit the Davidic or Mosaic patterns typically found in the messianic expectations of the time, this method of entry into Jerusalem was created by the church to fulfill a prophecy and not something that really happened.[1] However, it is possible that Jesus decided on this course of action precisely because it was *not* based on these well-known patterns. By his actions, Jesus may have been challenging these notions of the Messiah.

Jesus may have deliberately planned his entrance but this doesn't mean it was intended as the fulfillment of a prophecy. His actions in Jerusalem that Passover were probably intended as a parabolic teaching, rather than a fulfillment of prophecy a la Matthew and the early church.

Matthew 21.10-11 records the response of Jerusalem as follows: "When he entered Jerusalem, the whole city was in turmoil, asking, 'Who is this?' The crowds were saying, 'This is the prophet Jesus from Nazareth in Galilee.'" Matthew is exaggerating here, but this doesn't mean the description of Jesus as a prophet has no historical basis or that Jesus wasn't greeted by a crowd when he got to Jerusalem. Also, if Jesus was seen as a prophet it doesn't necessarily mean people saw him as *just* a prophet; the title could messianic in nature, with the meaning of "Jesus *the* prophet."

If Jesus did in fact ride into Jerusalem on a donkey, it seems likely that he was making a messianic statement. After all, the word that jumps out at you from Zechariah 9.9 is "king." We should note that the crowds are shouting about the "coming kingdom" of David, which is a response with definite messianic overtones.

The people around Jesus may have thought he was going to establish David's kingdom, but Jesus had a surprise in store for those who thought he was coming to Jerusalem as a Davidic king who would reestablish Israel's sovereignty.

Jesus' entry into Jerusalem probably got the attention of many—including the Romans and those in charge of the temple. If it didn't, what followed next certainly did. After his entry into Jerusalem, Jesus went to the temple and, according to Mark 11.15-16:

> ...he entered the temple and began to drive out those who were selling and those who were buying in the temple, and he overturned the tables of the money changers and the seats of those who sold doves; and he would not allow anyone to carry anything through the temple.

The description of this incident given in Matthew 21.12 is essentially the same as Mark's. Luke has a tendency to tone things down a little and omits the part about Jesus turning over tables and chairs. Luke 19.45 simply says that Jesus, "began to drive out those who were selling things." John 2.15 tells us that Jesus made a whip of cords and drove out the sheep and cattle being sold on the temple grounds.

In Matthew and Luke, Jesus cleanses the temple immediately upon entering Jerusalem. In Mark he does it the next day.

Most discussions of the cleansing don't provide many

details about the temple complex, but to understand this episode it is important to be familiar with the temple's layout. The temple was situated within four outer walls and the enclosed rectangular area was rather large. The western and eastern walls were the longest—both were over 1,500 feet long—while the northern and southern walls were each around 1,000 feet in length.[2] The animals were sold at the northern end of the temple grounds, while the money changers were found at the southern end. Thus, the temple grounds were large—longer than five football fields and wider than three. The temple itself took up perhaps a third of this total area, and was located roughly in the middle of the grounds.

The money changers in the temple have traditionally been seen as villains, but in Jesus' time they were there primarily as a convenience to those paying the annual temple tax. This tax was typically paid in Tyrian coinage, the most commonly used in Palestine at the time, and individuals with Roman and other coins would exchange them for the Tyrian silver pieces before paying the tax.

The temple grounds would have been very crowded with pilgrims and others around the time of the Passover, and there were probably *lots* of animals in the area. One source mentions 3,000 animals being brought to the temple to be sold for offerings on one occasion, although such a large number of animals may not have been present within the temple complex itself at one time.[3]

When we consider the size of the area involved, and the number of people and animals present at the time, it is hard to imagine that Jesus was physically able to do the things the Gospels describe without any help. Given the size of the temple grounds and the response by the authorities that his actions provoked, it is likely that Jesus acted in concert with his disciples, and that they essentially forced temple activities to a halt. It seems unlikely that Jesus tried to drive out a large number of animals in the temple area with crowds all around. This would have been a little too reckless. It is more plausible that Jesus and his disciples disrupted the trading in animals without actually trying to herd them out with whips. They probably didn't try to evict the money changers by force either, although turning over their tables seems within the realm of possibility.

At this point we need to face the big question regarding the cleansing: Why didn't the temple police or the Roman troops stationed nearby in the Antonia fortress intervene? The Antonia fortress was situated along the outside of the northern temple wall, and it would have taken only a matter of minutes for the cohort there to enter the temple grounds. Some believe Jesus' activity created a disturbance that was too big for them to control so they waited it out. Alternatively, some believe the cleansing might have been something so insignificant that they didn't feel the need to act. However, would Jesus have been executed by the Romans if he hadn't caused a major disturbance? I doubt it. I believe the Romans *did* intervene and that Jesus was arrested, not while praying in a garden at night, but in the temple at the time of the cleansing. It is likely that the Roman soldiers and temple police clashed with Jesus' followers, that Jesus wasn't the only person arrested, and that the men who were crucified with him were involved in the melee that broke out when the soldiers arrived.

We are accustomed to thinking that Jesus was "handed over" to the authorities peacefully, but the Gospels imply the arrest was a violent affair in which the disciples, and possibly other supporters of Jesus, fought with the arresting party. The synoptic Gospels contain a somewhat strange statement that, as Matthew 26.51 puts it, "one of those with Jesus" cut off the ear of the high priest's slave. The statement is strange because it doesn't refer to "a disciple," but to "one of those with Jesus." Although John 18.10 identifies Peter as the man with the sword, the wording of the synoptic Gospels may be a clue that "nondisciples" were present at the arrest. Also, from reading the Gospel accounts you'd think everyone was just standing around when this man lost his ear. I doubt that it happened that way, though. It is more likely that a scuffle broke out at the time of the arrest, regardless of where it took place. When they failed to protect Jesus, the disciples ran and went into hiding out of fear that they might be punished for their role in the incident.

In the descriptions given of the arresting party we find hints that Jesus' arrest may have occurred in the temple. In Matthew 26.47, Jesus is arrested by a large crowd carrying swords and clubs that has been sent by the "chief priests and elders of the people." In Mark 14.43 we find the same arresting party, except they have also come on behalf of "the scribes." These descriptions are consistent with a nighttime arrest. However, Luke 22.52 tells us that "the chief priests, the officers of the temple police, and the elders" *themselves* came out armed with swords and clubs to arrest Jesus, rather than delegating the task to subordinates. In John 18.3, Jesus is arrested by a "detachment of soldiers together with police from the chief priests and the Pharisees." This "detachment" is a cohort of Roman soldiers, which typically consisted of 600 men. So, while the accounts aren't consistent, I think Luke and John tell us the truth about who actually arrested Jesus—the temple police, the Roman cohort from the Antonia fortress, and the "chief priests" of the temple themselves. If this is who arrested Jesus, it seems likely that the arrest took place in the temple.

Since John's Gospel explicitly states the Romans were involved in Jesus' arrest, it isn't surprising that he moved the cleansing to the beginning of Jesus' ministry. John also seems to skip over the temple incident and move on to other things when he mentions it. By moving this event to the beginning of Jesus' ministry and then treating it as something insignificant, John has apparently attempted to sever the connection between the cleansing and the arrest in his Gospel.

It was probably at the time of the cleansing when Jesus made his comment to the effect that, "I will destroy this temple and build another, not made with human hands." This comment is recorded as one of the "false" charges against Jesus in his trial in Mark 14.58, and has been the subject of endless commentary and speculation. The author of John's Gospel thought Jesus was referring to his body, which would be resurrected, and most Christians today interpret the statement this way. However, I believe Jesus was predicting (1) the temple's destruction and (2) the establishment of the "temple" of the kingdom of God. Most people focus on what they think Jesus was saying *he* would do, but I believe Jesus was talking about what *God* was going to do. Jesus was pronouncing God's judgment on Israel for ignoring his prophetic message of repentance, and his hope for Israel's subsequent redemption.

With his statement of destroying and rebuilding the temple, Jesus may well have been heaping scorn on the temple reconstruction currently underway in his time. Herod had replaced Zerubbabel's temple with a grand, hellenistic monument that Jesus must have seen as an affront to God.

To understand what Jesus meant by the rebuilding of the temple it might help to look at something he says in John's Gospel, when he talks with the Samaritan woman by Jacob's well. I don't accept the historicity of the entire conversation, but one part of it seems relevant (John 4.19-21, 23-24):

> The woman said to him, "Sir, I see that you are a prophet. Our ancestors worshiped on this mountain, but you say that the place where people must worship is in Jerusalem." Jesus said to her, "Woman, believe me, the hour is coming when you will worship the Father neither on this mountain nor in Jerusalem.... But the hour is coming, and is now here, when the true worshipers will worship the Father in spirit and truth, for the Father seeks such as these to worship him. God is spirit, and those who worship him must worship in spirit and truth."

Jesus viewed Israel is the true "temple" of God. He didn't

see Herod's hellenistic monstrosity in Jerusalem as the temple any more than Christians see the buildings in which they meet as the church. This is why, when Jesus sent out the twelve disciples to Israel, he instructed them, per Matthew 10.9, to "Take no gold, or silver, or copper in your belts, no bag for your journey, or two tunics, or sandals, or a staff." These were essentially the same instructions given to Pharisaic pilgrims as they entered the temple.[4] Jesus was redefining the center of Jewish worship. He called upon his followers to worship God, not in a particular physical place, but in spirit and truth. For Jesus, the temple, or the kingdom of God, was equivalent to the people of Israel living in accordance with God's will.

We should stop to consider one important point here: How was this bombshell of a message about the impending destruction of the temple received by the crowds that were listening to Jesus? Was this what they expected to hear? Did they see this message as a hopeful one? Hardly. Like the disciples they were hoping for the dawn of a new, glorious age. Instead, Jesus dashed their hopes with a call to repentance and a prophecy that the temple would be destroyed. This was not what anyone in Jerusalem wanted to hear. This prediction of the temple's destruction would have been a threat to those in Jerusalem whose livelihoods depended on its operation, and a significant portion of the city's population would have fit into this category.[5] The Gospels tell us that many of the people turned against Jesus at the time of his crucifixion and it isn't hard to understand why—they wanted deliverance from heaven, but Jesus told them turn to God or face his judgment.

The scenario I've outlined above doesn't have much of a place for Judas' betrayal of Jesus. This matter isn't very significant. However, it is possible that, if Jesus was arrested with some others, Judas may have been among them, and he may have cooperated with the authorities to identify Jesus in exchange for his life.

I might add that the location of Jesus' arrest isn't really

important for understanding his life and ministry. I'm not trying to give the idea of the arrest occurring in the temple a hard sell; I just think it is a realistic possibility. Given the defensive, polemical nature of the traditions about Jesus' arrest and death, it wouldn't surprise me if the accounts of the cleansing and the arrest were separated for apologetic reasons.

Jesus' actions in the temple have traditionally been seen as a type of cleansing. The temple seemed to be in continual need of cleansing because it was defiled on a regular basis throughout its history. During the reign of Hezekiah the Levites cleansed the temple after it had been defiled by Ahaz (2 Chronicles 29.15); Josiah cleansed it by removing Manasseh's altars of the Baals (2 Chronicles 34.4); and Nehemiah cleansed the temple by throwing out the "household furniture" of Tobiah (Nehemiah 13.4-9). The temple was defiled not only by Israelite or Jewish rulers, but by foreigners as well. Examples include the desecration by Antiochus Epiphanes in 168 BCE, when a statue of Zeus was put in the temple, or Pompey's examination of the holy of holies in 63 BCE. The defilement of the temple and its cleansing, either through destruction or by some less drastic action, were concerns for many of the prophets.

It is often asserted that, with his actions, Jesus protested the "commercialization" of the temple, but we should avoid using this twentieth century concept to understand this episode. When we say something has been commercialized, we see a misplaced emphasis on its commercial aspects. Jesus may not have been challenging a misplaced commercial emphasis, but the presence of commerce in the temple altogether. As discussed earlier, Jesus did not have a high opinion of money in general, and he probably saw its use in the temple as a sign of corruption. Jesus believed forgiveness, ritual purity, entrance into the kingdom of God, could not be bought or earned.

It has been suggested that Jesus' actions in the temple constituted nothing more than a symbolic cleansing since he didn't attempt to establish any long-lasting reforms of cultic practices. It has also been suggested that he tried to ignite a rebellion against Rome, and ran with his disciples after the hoped-for insurrection didn't materialize. But Jesus wasn't stupid and he wasn't a coward. He knew that, sooner or later, he would be killed just like John the Baptist, and he came to Jerusalem to die. Jesus' death was his last parable, but it wasn't just some kind of symbolic protest. With his death he not only condemned the temple establishment, but provided his people with a graphic portrayal of where political messianism would lead them. The crucifixion completed the instruction that began with the triumphal entry.

The synoptic Gospels portray the cleansing as a prediction of judgment and doom. For Mark, the cleansing is a sign of God's rejection of Israel. He makes this clear by bracketing the incident with Jesus' cursing of the fig tree (which stands for Israel), and its subsequent withering. Matthew, which has the most Jewish orientation of all the Gospels, doesn't bracket the cleansing with the fig tree episode as Mark does; he puts the incident after the cleansing. This lessens the connection but doesn't sever it. Luke doesn't even mention Jesus cursing the fig tree, but there is no need—he puts an explicit prediction of Jerusalem's destruction directly in front of the cleansing.

As the church became a Gentile institution it saw the cleansing of the temple as a sign that God had rejected Israel. This was how it made sense of the traumatic events of the first century: Jerusalem was destroyed by the Romans; Christianity's founding church in Jerusalem and its mission to Israel failed; both Christians and Jews were persecuted by the Romans during the second half of the first century; and the church and the Pharisees took off the gloves in a desperate fight for survival. These events have left an indelible mark on the Gospel narratives, particularly the accounts of Jesus' arrest, trial and crucifixion.

The Trial of Jesus

The various accounts of Jesus' trial differ in minor details, but they all seem motivated by the desire to blame the Jewish people for the death of Jesus, and to show that the Romans didn't really view Jesus as a threat even though they crucified him as an insurrectionist. As a result, the accounts seem a little unrealistic.

It seems unlikely that Jesus was tried at the high priest's house, as Matthew 26.57 tells us. Luke suggests Jesus was detained in the high priest's house overnight until being questioned by the Sanhedrin the next morning. This seems just as improbable. In view of priests' alleged fear of the crowds, would the high priest have risked some type of disturbance at his home by bringing Jesus there? I can see the arresting party stopping by for a minute to report, but anything more seems unlikely.

Matthew 26.59-60 and Mark 14.57-59 tell us that false witnesses were brought before the Sanhedrin to testify, but that they could not agree. How likely is it that false witnesses produced at this "trial" would not be able to agree? The whole concept doesn't make sense. Perhaps this is why Luke and John left out this detail.

The exchange at the trial between Jesus and his accusers concerning Jesus' identity seems completely unrealistic. Luke's version is as follows (Luke 22.67-70):

> They said, "If you are the Messiah, tell us." He replied, "If I tell you, you will not believe; and if I question you, you will not answer. But from now on the Son of Man will be seated at the right hand of the power of God." All of them asked, "Are you, then, the Son of God?" He said to them, "You say that I am."

It seems that the language of the early church has been put into the mouths of Jesus' accusers. After all, in Mark's

Gospel even Jesus' closest disciples never figured out he was the Son of God, but in Luke the whole Sanhedrin seems to have made this connection! This identification of the Messiah, the Son of Man and the Son of God is something that was developed by the early church, not by the Sanhedrin at Jesus' trial.

Jesus' messianic claim might not have been considered blasphemy at the time of his execution. The statement about being exalted at the right hand of God might have seemed blasphemous only after Jesus' crucifixion since, per Deuteronomy 21.23, "anyone hung on a tree is under God's curse." Jesus wasn't killed because the Sanhedrin thought he was guilty of blasphemy. He was killed because the Romans saw the triumphal entry and the subsequent disturbance in the temple as the precursor of an insurrection. The temple establishment was involved also, but once the decision was made to arrest Jesus things happened quickly and the Romans were in charge the whole time.

Even though Jesus was executed by the Romans as a political threat, the account of Jesus' appearance before Pilate in Luke 23.3-4 is given as follows:

> Then Pilate asked him, "Are you the king of the Jews?" He answered, "You say so." Then Pilate said to the chief priests and the crowds, "I find no basis for an accusation against this man."

These are probably the most absurd verses in the account of Jesus' trial. Jesus basically affirms that he is "king of the Jews" but Pilate can't find a reason to accuse him!

When Pilate offers to release Jesus, since he can't find a reason to execute him, the synoptic Gospels have the Jews pick a bandit named Barabbas instead. Luke has Pilate try to convince the people that they really want Jesus, and the crowd keeps shouting, "crucify him, crucify him." As Pilate washes his hands of Jesus' blood, Matthew 27.25 has the crowd take full responsibility for Jesus' death with the words, "His blood be on us and on our children!" John 19.4-16 has a terrified Pilate practically beg the Jews to release Jesus, their king, and the temple priests respond by saying, "We have no king but the emperor" (John 19.15). The attempt to implicate "the Jews" in the death of Jesus has become a spectacle.

It should be noted that Pontius Pilate was a harsh man who tended to be somewhat heavy-handed in his treatment of the Jews. There were several incidents in which he threatened, attacked or executed Jews or Samaritans with little provocation. In fact, it may have been this ruthless treatment which eventually led to his recall to Rome in 36 CE. Pilate was also a very shrewd individual, as evidenced by the fact that he was governor of Judea for ten years, but it is hard to imagine him agonizing over the execution of a rebellious Galilean, or begging a crowd of Jews to have mercy on someone brought to him as an insurrectionist.

After the fall of the Jerusalem in 70 CE, the story of Barabbas was probably convincing to people in the Roman empire who were familiar with the Roman-Jewish war, during which Zealots or their sympathizers took over the temple and led the rebellion. The choice of Barabbas would be a good way to portray the Jewish people as enamored of bandits, since it would at least appear to be consistent with recent history. However, I doubt that anyone named Barabbas ever existed, or that Pilate ever pleaded with a Jewish mob to let Jesus go. It is just too incredible.

It doesn't seem likely that the first followers of Jesus knew what happened between the arrest and the crucifixion. Many of the things described in the accounts could not possibly have been witnessed by anyone and the disciples were on the run at the time. I don't think there was a trial at all. The high priest and his associates may have questioned Jesus after his arrest, but a final decision to execute Jesus was probably made before he was even arrested. The decision was made by the Romans, in consultation with the temple authorities, and I doubt there were any second thoughts. It was probably a quick, brutal affair.

As Christianity spread through the Roman empire, the execution of Jesus by the Romans was a constant problem. It led to suspicion that the new religion was subversive, and many hardships for the church. The Gospel accounts of the arrest and trial clearly go overboard trying to make the Jewish people responsible for Jesus' death, and to show that Christianity is not the threat it was taken to be.

The Crucifixion

The accounts we have of the crucifixion in the Gospels are extremely brief. In Matthew, only thirty verses take us from Pilate washing his hands of Jesus' blood to Joseph of Arimathea's request for Jesus' body. Mark uses only twenty, Luke uses twenty-three, and John gives the crucifixion thirty-seven verses.

Although the crucifixion accounts are brief, they are packed with details. As is usually the case, the details aren't always consistent. The details of the crucifixion, however, aren't particularly important for understanding the life of Jesus. There are only a few matters relating to the crucifixion that I would like to discuss.

In Matthew, Mark and John, Jesus is abused by the Roman soldiers. As this happens, the entire cohort that appeared in John's account of the arrest shows up in Matthew 27.27 and Mark 15.16. Matthew tells us that the cohort "gathered around" Jesus. This might not be a reference to the arrest, but, then, it might be.

The soldiers put a crown of thorns on Jesus' head, put a robe on him (scarlet in Matthew but purple in Mark and John) and hail him as "King of the Jews." From the mockery of these soldiers it is clear why Jesus is to be executed—the charge is political in nature. All four Gospels agree Jesus' cross had an inscription on it saying he was "King of the Jews." Jesus has done something which led to this accusation and the manner of his entry into Jerusalem may have had something to do with it.

Given that, as I've mentioned previously, the words of the onlookers at the crucifixion are based on Psalms 22, it seems possible that certain other details of the crucifixion are reconstructions of events as well, and not descriptions of the way things actually happened. I'm thinking particularly of the number and location of the "bandits" crucified with Jesus. For all we know there may have been ten or twenty. Also, maybe Jesus was placed at one end, rather than in the middle. It makes for a more powerful image to have three with Jesus in the middle, but that is just what makes me wonder if it really happened that way.

Matthew and Mark give identical accounts of Jesus' last words: "My God, my God, why have you forsaken me?" In Luke 23.46, Jesus' last words are, "Father, into your hands I commend my spirit." In John 19.28, Jesus says "I am thirsty." After receiving the sour wine, he says, in John 19.30, "It is finished," and then dies. Although they can't all have been his last words, Jesus could have said all of these things. In these words, we see a contrast between anguish and pain on the one hand, and peace and rest on the other. On the cross, Jesus sums up the spiritual history of humankind in a few words.

Was Jesus a Political Revolutionary?

The fact that Jesus was executed by the Romans on a political charge has led some to wonder if he intended to instigate a rebellion during the Passover. A number of factors are cited as support for this notion, besides the nature of the charge itself: (1) Jesus' message of the "kingdom of God" is inherently political. (2) In the Gospels Jesus never has anything negative to say about the Zealots, while the Pharisees get grilled for their hypocrisy. The reasoning goes that, if Jesus had said anything derogatory about Jews who supported armed revolution against the Romans, we would have heard about it. (3) Jesus picked a festival celebrating freedom from a foreign power as the time for his Jerusalem appearance. (4) Some see indications of armed resistance in the brief references to swords in Luke 22.35-38, and the armed resistance of the disciples at the time of Jesus' arrest. (5) Jesus' response to the question about paying taxes to Caesar can be seen as a statement that tribute based on the economy of Palestine should not be paid since this belongs to God.

Some advocates of the political revolution theory speculate that Jesus lost his stomach for insurrection after his failure to take over the temple, and that Judas turned Jesus in as he was trying to make his way out of Jerusalem under cover of darkness. Gethsemane, in this view, was a rendezvous point used by the revolutionaries.

I find these speculations interesting, but unconvincing. The evidence that Jesus advocated an armed insurrection is just so meager. However, I don't think we should assume that Jesus approved of the Roman presence in Judea. Certainly, he wanted them out of Palestine just like the rest of his countrymen, but I don't think the evidence for a political solution to the problem can be found in Jesus' teaching or his actions.

7

THE RESURRECTION

The Burial of Jesus

All four Gospels say that Joseph of Arimathea buried Jesus, but they seem a little uncomfortable with this man. Mark 15.43 says Joseph was "a respected member of the council, who was also himself waiting expectantly for the kingdom of God." Mark doesn't say that Joseph is a follower of Jesus, but simply implies it. Matthew 27.57 explicitly states that Joseph is a disciple of Jesus, and also tells us that Joseph is rich. Luke 23.50-51 tells us that, although he was a member of the council, Joseph "had not agreed to their plan and action." Luke also repeats Mark's statement about Joseph waiting for the kingdom. John 19.38 says that Joseph "was a disciple of Jesus, though a secret one because of his fear of the Jews." Obviously, Joseph wasn't the kind of disciple you need to have around when you are in trouble, because he apparently went along with Sanhedrin's decision to condemn Jesus without even speaking up. So, for obvious reasons, two of the Gospels seem reluctant to call Joseph a disciple, while the other two feel compelled to tell us why, as a member of the Sanhedrin, he didn't speak out in Jesus' defense during the trial.

After his apparent cowardice in the face of his countrymen, maybe Joseph wanted to make up for things by at least burying Jesus. Since he is rich and a member of the Sanhedrin he gets an audience with Pilate and asks him for Jesus' body. There is no doubt about it—this took guts. The first question Pilate would be likely to ask is: "Are you this man's follower?" Joseph could well have been risking crucifixion himself by approaching Pilate, though his money and position might have offered him protection that Jesus didn't have. So here we have a man who wouldn't stand up to the Sanhedrin, but is willing to risk his life by coming before Pilate under his own initiative and asking for Jesus' body.

This request of Joseph is inconsistent with the attempt of the "chief priests and Pharisees" to prevent Jesus' followers from stealing his body in Matthew 27.62-66. Where were these people the day before, when Joseph was asking Pilate for the body? Why did they wait until Jesus had been buried by Joseph to show an interest in preventing the disciples from stealing Jesus' body? Why did they wait until the sabbath to make their request? Something isn't right here.

We might also ask how the chief priests and Pharisees figured out that Jesus would rise from the dead after three days. After all, the disciples couldn't figure this out after being told by Jesus on three separate occasions. If the chief priests and Pharisees had known anything about the disciples they wouldn't have worried since, after the crucifixion, when the women came to tell the disciples that Jesus had risen, they thought the women's story was "an idle tale" (Luke 24.11).

It has been suggested that Mark portrays Joseph as a pious Jew who just wanted to take down the crucified men (Jesus and the two others) so their bodies would not be hanging on the crosses during the Passover festival. However, Mark makes no reference to Joseph asking for the bodies of the other two men. It has also been suggested that the details related to the burial of the other two individuals were ignored because they weren't important. I don't find this argument very convincing. Did Joseph know of three tombs, one for each of the men? Did all three men die after three hours on the cross? Did Joseph have time to bury all three? Isn't this a little bit too much? I find it more likely that Mark saw Joseph as a disciple or follower of Jesus. In reality, however, I think Joseph is a purely fictitious character.

The descriptions of the tomb and burial in the Gospels are designed to show that Jesus' tomb could be located and that his body would not be confused with someone else's. However, the descriptions get better and better as we go from Mark to John. In Mark 15.46, it is simply "a tomb that had been hewn out of rock" with a stone rolled in front of the door. In Matthew 27.60 it is Joseph's own, personal tomb and it is new. In John 19.41 it is in a garden to boot. Having such a nice tomb so near the site of the crucifixion seems just a little convenient to me.

The manner of burial exhibits a similar development: it goes from the hurried to the regal. In Mark 15.46, Jesus is simply tied up in a linen cloth by Joseph. By the time we get to John 19.39-40, Joseph, with the help of Nicodemus, uses a hundred pounds of myrrh and aloes to embalm the body.

One scholar has stated that, "We have seen in the canonical Gospels a line of development that moved Joseph from being a pious Sanhedrist observing the law of burying the crucified toward a more sanctified status as a model disciple of Jesus."[1] This is a good description of the development of the Easter story in microcosm: a steady enrichment and ennoblement of the entire affair by Jesus' followers. The Gospels show a consistent tendency to make things bigger and better, with the result that the burial stories appear implausible and contradictory.

It is more likely that Jesus was buried by the Romans after his crucifixion and that Jesus' followers never knew where he was buried. In John 20.13, Mary Magdalene says to an angel at the empty tomb, "They have taken away my Lord, and I do not know where they have laid him." Then, in John 20.15, Mary is speaking to the risen Christ, whom she mistakes for "the gardener," and she says, "Sir, if you have carried him away, tell me where you have laid him, and I will take him away." These sound like words that might have been spoken to the Romans in charge of the crucifixion, rather than to angels or the risen Christ.

In Acts 13.28-30, Paul is preaching and he says:

> Even though they found no cause for a sentence of death, they asked Pilate to have him killed. When they had carried out everything that was written about him, they took him down from the tree and laid him in a tomb. But God raised him from the dead.

In these verses Paul actually says that the men who crucified Jesus took him down from the cross and buried him. He says nothing about Joseph of Arimathea. This is probably closer to the truth than the Gospel accounts.

The Resurrection Accounts

Of the four Gospels, Mark has the briefest account of the resurrection—he gives it only eight verses. The Gospel apparently ended at Mark 16.8, with the two Marys running from the empty tomb in terror after seeing a "young man, dressed in a white robe" (Mark 16.5). Although the young man instructs them to tell the disciples Jesus will "go ahead" of them into Galilee, Mark says, "they said nothing to anyone, for they were afraid" (Mark 16.8).

As noted earlier, this abrupt, unsatisfactory ending was too much, or rather too little, for the early church to handle and a couple of more suitable endings were attached later.

Matthew gives the most important event in history a grand total of twenty verses. The same two women go to the tomb, and they see an angel descend from heaven and roll back the stone. No mention is made of a young man dressed in white, but the angel's message to the two women is essentially the same as the young man's in Mark. This time, however, the women are afraid but they also have "great joy." As they are leaving, the two women meet Jesus, who greets them and repeats the angel's message.

When the disciples see Jesus in Galilee, he gives them the "great commission," in which he tells them to, "...make disciples of all nations, baptizing them in the name of the Father and of the Son and of the Holy Spirit..." (Matthew 28.19). Matthew 28.17 tells us that, as the disciples worshipped Jesus, "some doubted."

Matthew provides the little tidbit that the guards at the tomb were paid to tell everyone that Jesus' body was stolen by his disciples, and that "this story is still told among the Jews to this day" (Matthew 28.15). This lets us know that, when Matthew wrote, the resurrection wasn't something that had happened recently.

Luke gives the resurrection fifty-three verses, and his Gospel is the only one to tell us of the ascension. Luke tells us that a number of women came to the tomb, and that they saw "two men in dazzling clothes" (Luke 24.4). The women then go to the disciples, who are thoroughly skeptical about their story. Only Peter bothers to go to the tomb to check it out!

Luke tells us how Jesus appears to two disciples as they are walking to Emmaus, a small town outside of Jerusalem. They don't recognize Jesus until he breaks bread with them, and he disappears as soon as they realize who he is. These disciples then meet the eleven, and as they are being informed that Jesus had appeared to Peter, Jesus is suddenly standing in their midst. He eats a piece of broiled fish to show his disciples he isn't a ghost. Unlike Mark and Matthew, where Jesus is to meet the disciples in Galilee, in Luke, Jesus tells the disciples to remain in Jerusalem until the Holy Spirit comes. He then ascends to heaven as he is walking with the disciples to Bethany.

John's resurrection account takes up the thirty-one verses of chapter 20, and as much of chapter 21 as you are willing to consider related to the resurrection.

In John's account, only Mary Magdalene comes to the empty tomb. When she sees it is empty she immediately runs to tell Peter and the beloved disciple (John 20.2). It is only after Mary returns to the tomb that she sees two angels, and then sees Jesus, whom she mistakes for the gardener. Jesus later suddenly appears to the disciples in a locked room, then has Thomas touch his wounds to show him he is real. Thomas' perplexity seems warranted, since real people don't usually just walk through solid walls.

The 21st chapter of John tells of an appearance by Jesus in Galilee, where he helps the disciples catch and eat some fish.

Given the monumental importance of the resurrection, the brevity and inconsistency of the Gospel accounts are stunning. Matthew says there was a guard at the tomb, while the other three Gospels omit this detail. Mark says there was one young man at the tomb, while Luke says there were two. Matthew has one angel; John has two angels. Mark and Matthew place the two Marys at the tomb, John has one, while Luke has a group of women there. In Matthew and Mark, Jesus appears, or is to appear, to the disciples in Galilee while, in Luke, Jesus *never* appears to the disciples there. In fact, he orders them to remain in Jerusalem. These inconsistencies don't mean the resurrection didn't take place, but they don't inspire confidence either.

Women play a prominent role in each of the accounts. They are the first to the tomb and tell the disciples of Jesus' resurrection. Since the disciples weren't present at the crucifixion, they probably relied on the women for information about what happened to Jesus after he was taken down from the cross.

In Luke and John, the importance of the scriptures for understanding Jesus' death and resurrection is emphasized. At first, the disciples "did not understand the scripture, that he must rise from the dead" (John 20.9). Luke tells us that when he spoke to the disciples after his resurrection, "he opened their minds to understand the scriptures" (Luke 24.45). This tells us that, after his death, Jesus' disciples searched the scriptures in an attempt to make sense of what had happened.

Two other features of the resurrection accounts are interesting. These are the apparent inability of people to recognize Jesus after his resurrection and the doubts among the disciples that are mentioned. Perhaps these things imply that some of the disciples never accepted the resurrection story. Clearly, according to Luke, *none* of them did at first. It is possible that not all of Jesus' disciples "saw" him after his death.

What Really Happened?

If we assume that the resurrection didn't actually happen as the Bible records it—with an empty tomb, angels descending from heaven, and Jesus ascending to heaven on a cloud afterwards—we need to look at what might have happened to the disciples that made them believe Jesus had risen. In order to do this we should look, not at "the eleven," but at Paul's encounter with the risen Christ, which is described in Acts 9.3-9 as follows:

Now as he was going along and approaching Damascus, suddenly a light from heaven flashed around him. He fell to the ground and heard a voice saying to him, "Saul, Saul, why do you persecute me?" He asked, "Who are you, Lord?" the reply came, "I am Jesus, whom you are persecuting. But get up and enter the city, and you will be told what you are to do." The men who were traveling with him stood speechless because they heard the voice but saw no one. Saul got up from the ground, and though his eyes were open, he could see nothing; so they led him by the hand and brought him into Damascus. For three days he was without sight, and neither ate nor drank.

Paul doesn't describe an experience like this in his letters. In Galatians 1.15-17, he says that God "was pleased to reveal his Son to me" (or "in me"). In Philippians 3.21, he says Christ will "transform our humble bodies that [they] may be conformed to his glorious body" (NRSV alternative translation). These are probably references to his own vision of the risen Christ. Nowhere does he mention losing his sight for three days or seeing a light from heaven.

From his letters and the information provided by Acts it appears Paul had many powerful spiritual experiences. In 2 Corinthians 12.1-4, Paul talks of being "caught up to the third heaven—whether in the body or out of the body I do not know." With reference to this experience Paul speaks of "visions and revelations of the Lord." In Galatians 2.2, Paul says he went to Jerusalem "in response to a revelation." In Acts 22.17-18, Paul is reported to have said, "while I was praying in the temple, I fell into a trance and saw Jesus."

It seems probable, based on these descriptions of Paul's experiences, that what he saw as an appearance of the risen Christ was some type of ecstatic vision. Paul's experiences lack the physical characteristics of the resurrection in the Gospels. It seems more appropriate to describe Paul's encounter with the risen Christ as something that happened to Paul, rather than something that happened to Jesus.

Paul saw his own experience as identical to the other resurrection appearances, as he indicates at 1 Corinthians 15.3-8:

> For I handed on to you as of first importance what I in turn had received: that Christ died for our sins in accordance with the scriptures, and that he was buried, and that he was raised on the third day in accordance with the scriptures, and that he appeared to Cephas, then to the twelve. Then he appeared to more than five hundred brothers and sisters at one time, most of whom are still alive, though some have died. Then he appeared to James, then to all the apostles. Last of all, as to one untimely born, he appeared also to me.

I agree with Paul when he puts his own experience of the risen Christ on the same level of the other appearances he mentions, but I believe all these events were visions or "revelations" of an ecstatic nature and not appearances of a physical, resurrected Jesus. This doesn't mean these experiences don't have some enduring spiritual reality behind them, but I believe the Gospels' resurrection accounts are fleshed-out legends based on the religious experiences of Jesus' earliest followers.

This explanation is unsatisfactory to people who think Jesus physically came back to life, ate broiled fish, and went to heaven on a cloud. They will become very upset by this because, they feel, it changes the story of Jesus from one of comfort and hope into a tragic one. In addition, to say that Jesus didn't rise from the dead makes it sound like Christianity is based on a lie. Although I can certainly understand these reactions, I don't agree with these views. First, every human being who has ever lived has died, or is going to die at some point in the future. Should we say that simply because Jesus died, his life was tragic? Only if you think life and death is a tragedy. Of course, the method of Jesus' death and the fact that he was deserted by practically everyone when it happened is certainly tragic, but Jesus chose his own path and lived his life in accordance with his deepest beliefs. For this we can be thankful. As for the idea that Christianity is somehow based on a lie, I think Christianity's basis is the transforming effect Jesus had on the lives of the people who knew him, not an empty tomb. Even if you believe that Jesus didn't rise from the dead, you can still love the man and want to be his servant. When he dies, will his disciples abandon him?

In Luke 10.18, Jesus says, "I watched Satan fall from heaven like a flash of lightning." With these words, Jesus describes something that happened, not during the first century, but at the beginning of time. He says he witnessed it. We are also present at the creation. This is the only moment, the original moment. We can't see this because, in the midst of this primeval forest, we are busy building a temple to ourselves. Jesus was able to see beyond our petty preoccupations, and he proclaimed what he saw as the dawning of God's kingdom. This is the basis upon which Christianity rests.

8

SOME PERSONAL THEOLOGICAL REFLECTIONS

I would like to conclude with some personal theological reflections. Often, when someone writes about the historical Jesus, I want to know something about the author's personal beliefs so I can see how they have dealt with the theological issues raised by the critical examination of Jesus' life. Consequently, I want to provide some my own personal beliefs to show how I've dealt with the questions raised in this book, and to shed some light on the kinds of assumptions I've brought to this endeavor.

I would like to start with some general observations about the world's major religions.

The world's major religions generally share four characteristics. First, they are provincial. By this I mean that they all insist on being right at everyone else's expense. One of the most provincial statements I've heard Christians make is the assertion that, "Religion is man's attempt to reach God; Christianity is God's attempt to reach man." This is what I mean by "provincial." It is saying, "We are right and everyone else is wrong."

Next, the major religions tend to be anthropocentric; they make what happens to humankind the center of the universe. Everything else fades into the background.

In addition to being anthropocentric, the major religions tend to be chauvinistic. In other words, they aren't just interested in what happens to humankind, they are specifically interested in what men do, and they understand the world with masculine terminology and images. For example, in Christianity, God is the "Father," and he has a "Son." You have to give the Catholics credit for letting Mary share the theological spotlight, but the world view of Christianity is, nonetheless, as chauvinistic as the next religion's.

Finally, the world's major religions tend to operate within the context of an antiquated world view. This is just because they've been around for a while, and people in modern industrial societies see the world much differently than people did hundreds or thousands of years ago.

As you might have guessed, I don't see the above characteristics of religion as positive attributes. These characteristics, together with the strong correlation between religious beliefs and cultural identity, often lead religion to become a divisive and oppressive force in human affairs. Unfortunately, we humans are so insecure that it takes little to make us feel threatened and become defensive, and we are fond of using our religions to support our territorial claims, both physical and "spiritual." We don't hesitate to invoke our religious beliefs when we use violence to take land from other nations, or to condemn or kill people who don't see things as we do. These abuses of religion are a sad commentary on human nature.

Despite our tendency to abuse our religions, they hold the key with which we can unlock the door to the source of our being. The choice of one's religion may be important, but the crucial thing is the willingness to take that key, open the door to what lies beyond, and walk through it. I don't think any one religion has a monopoly on the truth.

I believe there is a God, but my conception of God is very different from what is found in the Bible. I don't believe God gets jealous or angry. These are human emotions that should not be attributed to God. I don't believe God plays favorites. He doesn't intervene in history on behalf of one person or group of people at the expense of another.

Many people believe that the physical world is governed by "natural laws," and that God is a supernatural power who intervenes in history to reveal his will to humankind. When God acts in history, he often sets aside the natural laws that govern his creation and miraculous events result. These miracles are seen as signs of God's activity. Example include Jesus walking on water or raising the dead.

I don't accept this view of things. Miraculous events don't prove claims that individuals make about God, or mean that God has intervened in history. They simply mean that there are things we don't understand. That is all.

It is often said that, if you don't believe miracles are possible, you are doubting God's power. This is completely backwards—life itself is a miracle beyond our comprehension. Our fixation on the unusual and extraordinary is a measure of how desperate we have become, and how much we take for granted.

I don't believe God is masculine. I don't think he is some kind of glorified man. I don't think God is feminine, either. Of course, if we are to talk about God we have to refer to "Him" somehow. I often use masculine designations, but only because it is traditional. Sometimes I use language that sounds like I am calling God an "it" or a "thing," but this isn't meant to suggest that God is some kind of mechanical, impersonal force or being. It is just a recognition of the limits of our understanding and the inadequacy of language to express the inexpressible. In short, I think that God is a mystery beyond the reach of all our chauvinistic expressions.

In response to the anthropomorphic images of God in the Bible, some adopt a "deistic" view of God—they see God as impersonal and uninvolved with human affairs. This view isn't an improvement over the Bible's; it just demotes God from a glorified person to some kind of monolithic force or power that isn't interested in what happens to humans. I believe God is active in his creation in a global or universal sense, but also that he is active in the lives of individuals. However, the things that religious people like to attribute to God are usually the result of wishful thinking or pure fantasy, and we tread on dangerous spiritual ground whenever we start attributing motives or particular actions to God.

It is God's nature to become what he isn't. He is infinite, so he becomes what is finite. He is holy, so he becomes what is unholy. He is eternal, so he becomes that which is subject to change; he never dies, so he becomes all that lives and dies. In Christian terms, he is God, but becomes man; he is eternal and unchanging, but he dies on the cross; he is blameless, but is executed as a criminal.

God does not assert himself, but surrenders himself absolutely. This is the meaning of the incarnation, crucifixion and resurrection of Christ to me: Life is about giving away, not acquiring things, and this giving is what creates the universe. God's creative activity is not something that happened in the past; it is eternally present. This very moment is the creation of the universe.

We tend to understand God using concepts, but I don't think God has a voice or speaks to people. We simply understand what we experience (whether it is God or anything else) using language. At some point, though, our experience ceases to provide conceptual answers. You cannot fit the ocean into a cup. It is impossible put into words what happens when humans encounter God directly. Language and concepts don't rule or understand this realm of our existence.

I don't believe in heaven or hell. I don't believe in reincarnation either. Our desire for immortality is really just a measure of our indifference, our lack of appreciation for what we have been given. We are so busy running after things we don't have that we rarely take the time to appreciate just being alive. We forget what it is like to just put one foot in front of the other, or to just breathe in and out. This isn't good enough; we always want more.

People place so much importance on the idea of "life after death." It isn't just Christians either. Just about every religion has an expectation that life will continue in some way after death. However, people should stop to consider what they are saying when they talk about living or "going on" forever. Think for a second about living for billions and billions of years. Just think for a minute about life *never* ending. Does it even make sense? Is this really what we want? I know we *think* we want this, but do we really? Perhaps it is just that we want everything right now but can't have it.

We should also think in more mundane terms about what living forever would be like. What would eternity be like for people who have died as infants, or toddlers, and haven't lived long enough to develop a sense of separate identity? What about people who die when they are very old and feeble? What type of body will they, or we, have in the afterlife? Will we even have a body? Will we recognize each other? Jesus said that people don't marry in heaven, that family ties don't mean anything. What exactly *should* we expect? This is where the "I have to trust God" routine starts. I find this statement pops up any time the utter absurdity of our beliefs becomes apparent. We expect God to "make everything OK." We expect him to make us happy forever. Isn't this just a little childish?

When you consider the practical aspects of eternal life, it becomes clear that it involves something other than our ordinary sense of identity. After all, if we won't have our bodies, our memories, or the relationships that define who we are in this life, why do we insist that "we" will live forever? Even if we have all these things, but have somehow been "transformed" so that "everything is OK," will we even be the same person?

On the other hand, I don't believe that "we die when we die." While I don't believe we live forever in the storybook fashion, I believe there is an eternal dimension to our existence. What is this "eternal dimension?" I can't tell you. If I was an eagle, I could soar over the trees on the wind. I wouldn't have to sit at red lights or look at my watch. But I wouldn't have arms to hug my children with. We don't have to look far, and we don't have to wish for what we don't have.

We humans tend to see things in life as good or bad, as allies or enemies. Life isn't really like that, though. If you truly practice your religion—whatever it may be—you can reach a place in your life where you see that, in come indefinable sense, every event has the same shape. Then, you can greet everything that happens as you would an old friend. Behind the many voices that call you during a lifetime, you sense one primordial voice. When you come to this place there are no enemies. When death comes it isn't something to be vanquished, but just another old friend to be greeted.

Some people feel that, if we don't have the threat of judgment hanging over our heads, the law of the jungle will prevail. These people don't watch the evening news. The law of the jungle already prevails. People are restrained mostly by the expectations of others, not the expectation of judgment after they die. I believe we should do what is right without any expectation of a reward; doing the right thing is reward enough.

We humans take ourselves much too seriously. We think that we are at the center of things, and that the world revolves around what we think, believe, and do with our lives. This is an ego trip.

I can't discuss my personal religious beliefs without mentioning the Mahayana Buddhist ideal of the bodhisattva and how Jesus' life and teaching have affected my interpretation of this concept. A bodhisattva is a being who renounces Buddhahood, supreme enlightenment, release from the cycle of birth and death, etc., to help others reach liberation from suffering. This being vows to renounce his own liberation until all beings have attained Buddhahood. This is really an eternal vow to work on behalf of others. Buddhists tend to see bodhisattvas as very advanced, exalted spiritual beings—they are one step from becoming Buddhas. However, I believe bodhisattvas are found in the most unlikely places and our salvation lies where we least expect it. Bodhisattvas are the rejected, cast aside, ignored, mistreated things in this life. They are the children we abuse, the fragile, irreplaceable ecosystems we destroy for short-term profit, the animals we treat like machines and then eat, and the poor in our inner cities. They aren't "spiritually advanced" beings to be put on pedestals, but the ones that suffer needlessly and make human redemption possible; bodhisattvas are suffering servants, not glorified kings, and they are everywhere. The magnolia tree in my front yard is a bodhisattva, and the tree of life stands next to a road near my house.

You might have noticed that, so far, Jesus hasn't shown up in my inventory of personal beliefs. Who do I think Jesus was? When I look at his life I have to ask: What happens to a person who is a living archetype, or whose life is a kind of lightning rod collecting the hopes, dreams and the fears of billions of people? What happens when one life unfolds in a pattern that emits a powerful signal reaching the depths of the human spirit?

Let's suppose someone takes some pieces of paper about an inch square, each of which has a letter written on it. This person throws the printed letters in the air and they fall to the ground, scattered all about. The life of Jesus is like four of the letters falling together in a perfect line and spelling the word "love." Actually, everything that happens is like this, but sometimes one person's life can become a conduit through which this takes place, or through which this is revealed, and Jesus' life was like that.

Things seem to happen at random, and they do. At the same time, they happen according to a divine plan. These aren't mutually exclusive possibilities. Life is a series of powerful connections, of random events sending a message that is always present. We just are too busy watching ourselves to notice. Every once in a while, though, someone comes along who breaks through our cocoons. Jesus had that ability.

Most of us muddle through life. Things blend together, without enduring markers that chart our course. Sometimes, though, a person's life can be transformed by the actions or simple presence of another—not just changed a little or a lot, but truly transformed. Son of God, Lord, Messiah, King—these exalted titles and descriptions of Jesus didn't collect around him because he was in the right place at the right time, although he was. They gathered around him because he transformed people's lives. If you look closely at his life while looking closely at your own as well, he still can.

Endnotes

Chapter 1

1. Baruch Halpern, *The Emergence of Israel in Canaan* (Chico, CA: Scholars Press, 1983), 63.
2. See comments of Israel Finkelstein in *The Rise of Ancient Israel* (Washington: Biblical Archeological Society, 1992), 68.
3. Theodore H. Robinson, "The History of Israel," ed. George Arthur Buttrick et al., *The Interpreter's Bible* (Nashville: Abingdon Press, 1954), Volume 1, 275.
4. Ibid., 277-278.
5. Ibid., 278.
6. Neal Bierling, *Giving Goliath His Due* (Grand Rapids: Baker Book House, 1992), 89, 92.
7. Ibid., 151.
8. Robinson, op. cit., 280.
9. Ibid., 281.
10. Ibid., 282.
11. G.W. Anderson, *The History and Religion of Israel* (Oxford: Oxford University Press, 1966), 58.
12. Robinson, op. cit.
13. Ibid., 285.
14. Ibid., 286.
15. Rupert Furneaux, *The Roman Siege of Jerusalem* (New York: David McKay Company, Inc., 1972), 28.
16. Michael Grant, *The Jews in the Roman World* (New York: Charles Scribner's Sons, 1973), 25.
17. Ibid., 24.
18. Ibid., 25.
19. Ibid., 26.
20. Ibid., 27.
21. Ibid., 142.
22. Philip L. Culbertson, *A Word Fitly Spoken* (Albany: State University of New York Press, 1995), 73-74.
23. *The Jews in the Roman World*, 32.

24. Ibid., 66-67.
25. Ibid.
26. Gerd Theissen, *The First Followers of Jesus*, trans. John Bowden (London: SCM Press Ltd., 1978), 73.
27. David M. Rhoads, *Israel in Revolution: 6-74 C.E.* (Philadelphia:Fortress Press, 1976), 24-25.
28. Ibid., 28.
29. Ibid., 29.
30. *The Jews in the Roman World*, 60.
31. Ibid., 194-200.
32. Ibid., 201-202.
33. *The Jews in the Roman World*, 247-256.
34. William Scott Green, "Messiah in Judaism," ed. Jacob Neusner et al., *Judaisms and Their Messiahs and the Turn of the Christian Era* (Cambridge: Cambridge University Press, 1987), 3.
35. John J. Collins, *The Scepter and the Star: The Messiahs of the Dead Sea Scrolls and Other Ancient Literature* (New York: Doubleday, 1995), 40-41.
36. Kenneth E. Pomykala, *The Davidic Dynasty Tradition in Early Judaism* (Atlanta: Scholars Press, 1995), 268.
37. R.B. Wright trans., "The Psalms of Solomon," James H. Charlesworth ed., *The Old Testament Pseudepigrapha* (Garden City: Doubleday & Company, Inc., 1983), Volume 2, 667-668.
38. Howard M. Teeple, *The Mosaic Eschatological Prophet* (Philadelphia:Society of Biblical Literature, 1957), 100-101.
39. M.A. Knibb trans., "1 Enoch," ed. H.F.D. Sparks, *The Apocryphal Old Testament* (New York: Oxford University Press, 1984), 229.
40. Jerome Murphy-O'Connor, O.P., "Qumran and the New Testament," ed. Eldon Jay Epp and George W. MacRae, *The New Testament and its Modern Interpreters* (Atlanta: Society of Biblical Literature, 1989), 55-56.
41. John J. Collins, "The Son of Man in First-Century Judaism," *New Testament Studies* 38 (1992), 464-465.
42. David E. Aune, *Prophecy in Early Christianity and the Ancient Mediterranean World* (Grand Rapids: William B. Eerdmans Publishing Company, 1983), 127-128.
43. Sean Freyne, *Galilee from Alexander the Great to Hadrian*

(Wilmington, Del.: Michael Glazer, Inc., 1980), 3.

44. Michael Grant, *Jesus: An Historian's Review of the Gospels* (1977, New York: Touchstone Books, 1995), 73.

45. Ibid., 73-74.

46. Richard A. Horsley, *Sociology and the Jesus Movement* (New York: The Crossroad Publishing Company, 1989), 76.

47. Ibid., 77.

48. Neil Asher Silberman, "Searching for Jesus," *Archeology* (New York: Archeology Institute of America, 1994), November/December, 1994, 37.

49. Freyne, op. cit., 162-163.

50. Freyne, op. cit., 12-13.

51. Neil Asher Silberman, "The World of Paul," *Archeology* (New York: Archeological Institute of America, 1996), November/December 1996, 35.

52. Philip J. King, "Jerusalem," ed. David Noel Freedman et al., *The Anchor Bible Dictionary* (New York: Doubleday, 1992), Vol. 3, 753.

53. John Wilkinson, *Jerusalem As Jesus Knew It* (London: Thames and Hudson Ltd., 1978), 30-32.

54. Leibel Reznick, *The Holy Temple Revisited* (Northvale, NJ, London: Jason Aronson Inc., 1990), 11.

55. Martin Goodman, *The Ruling Class of Judaea* (Cambridge: Cambridge University Press, 1987), 65-66.

56. Martin Hengel, *The 'Hellenization' of Judaea in the First Century after Christ*, trans. John Bowden (London: SCM Press Ltd; Philadelphia: Trinity Press International, 1989), 10-11.

57. Joachim Jeremias, *Jerusalem in the Time of Jesus*, trans. F.H. and C.H. Cave (Philadelphia: Fortress Press, 1967), 5-9.

58. Ibid., 22-25.

59. Ibid., 45.

60. John Riches, "Sadducees," ed. Bruce M. Metzger and Michael D. Coogan, *The Oxford Companion to the Bible* (New York: Oxford University Press, 1993), 667-668.

61. Anthony J. Saldarini, "Pharisees," *The Anchor Bible Dictionary*, Volume 5, 302.

62. Richard A. Horsley, *Sociology and the Jesus Movement* (New York: Crossroad Publishing Company, 1989), 75.

63. Joseph A. Fitzmeyer, *Responses to 101 Questions on the Dead Sea Scrolls* (Mahwah, NJ: Paulist Press, 1992), 1-2.
64. Ibid., 2-4.
65. Ibid., 91.
66. Ibid., 101-102.
67. Ibid., 3-4.
68. Ibid., 54.
69. Ibid., 42-43.
70. Ibid., 107.
71. Ibid., 108.
72. Geza Vermes, *The Dead Sea Scrolls in English* (1962, New York: The Penguin Group, 1995), xx-xxi.

Chapter 2

1. Aune, op. cit., 231.
2. Ibid., 245.
3. Irving Jacobs, *The Midrashic Process*, (Cambridge: Cambridge University Press, 1995), 4.
4. Robert W. Funk et al., *The Five Gospels* (New York: Polebridge Press, 1993), 10-11.
5. Raymond E. Brown and John P. Meier, *Antioch & Rome* (Ramsey: Paulist Press, 1983), 27.
6. William E. Hull, John, ed. Clifton J. Allen et al., *Broadman Bible Commentary* (Nashville: Broadman Press, 1970), Volume 9, 199-200.
7. Ibid., 197-198.

Chapter 3

1. Donald A. Hagner, Matthew 1-13, ed. David A. Hubbard et al., *Word Biblical Commentary*, (Dallas: Word, Incorporated, 1993), Volume 33a, page 19.
2. Hengel, op. cit., 8.
3. Adela Yarbro Collins, "Daniel 7 and the Historical Jesus," ed. Harold W. Attridge et al., *Of Scribes and Scrolls* (Lanham, MA: University Press of America, 1990), 193.

Chapter 4

1. Hans Walther Wolff, "Prophecy from the Eighth Through the Fifth Century," trans. W. Sibley Towner and Joy E. Heebink, in James Luther Mays and Paul J. Achtemeier, ed., *Interpreting the Prophets* (Philadelphia: Fortress Press, 1987), 20-22.
2. Robert R. Wilson, "Early Israelite Prophecy," *Interpreting the Prophets*, 6.
3. Brad H. Young, *Jesus and His Jewish Parables* (Mahwah, NJ: Paulist Press, 1989), 3-5.
4. My analysis of this parable is indebted to Kenneth Ewing Bailey, *Poet and Peasant* (Grand Rapids: William B. Eerdmans Publishing Company, 1976), 86-110.
5. My analysis of this parable is based on the work of Kenneth Ewing Bailey in *Poet and Peasant*, 158-206.

Chapter 6

1. John Dominic Crossan, *Jesus: A Revolutionary Biography* (San Francisco: HarperSanFrancisco, 1994), 129.
2. Reznick, op. cit., 24.
3. Jeremias, op. cit., 49.
4. Bruce Chilton, *The Temple of Jesus* (University Park, PA: The Pennsylvania State University Press, 1992), 126.
5. Gerd Theissen, *Social Reality and the Early Christians* (Minneapolis: Fortress Press, 1992), Margaret Kohl trans., 109-112.

Chapter 7

1. Raymond E. Brown, *The Death of the Messiah* (New York: Doubleday, 1994), Volume 2, page 1232.